"Early Christians in the Roman Empire had a spectrum of experiences with Roman rule in general, and Roman centurions in particular. Mercer provides an accessible introduction to the role of centurions in the imperial army, thus helping us today get a sense of the lived experience of those who birthed the Jesus movement. He raises interesting questions about the inclusion of centurions in the biblical narrative, and provides some helpful pastoral commentary along the way."

Gordon L. Heath, PhD, FRHistS
Professor Christian History
Centenary Chair in World Christianity

"Steven Mercer's experience as a Green Beret serves him well as he deploys current military expressions ('tactical' versus 'strategic'; 'casualty rates'; 'duty rosters'; 'senior non-commissioned officers') to bring these Bible-times characters to life. And since, as he argues, centurions come off well in the New Testament, it's good for us to take a closer look at these men whom the Lord featured so prominently in the text. Drawing on an impressive collection of resources from both inside and outside the Church, Mercer artfully *explicates* ('Italian Cohort'), *delineates* (three different lessons from the three prominent centurions), *repudiates* (the notion that the centurion in Matthew 8 may have been a pederast), *illustrates* (through extra-biblical accounts of such centurions as Marcus Petronius and Aurelius Marcianus), and *speculates* (that Theophilus may have once been a centurion, and that the centurion at the foot of the cross may have been Herodian). Having read this book, I find that centurions jump off the page when I read Matthew, Luke, and Acts.

Mark Coppenger
Retired Professor of Christian Philosophy and Ethics,
The Southern Baptist Theological Seminary

"Steven Mercer offers a helpful resource for readers of Scripture. Who are the Roman Centurions? Mercer explores several descriptions within modern scholarship, early accounts of Centurions in ancient literature, and provides a close eye on the scriptural testimony. He combines both disciplines of historical studies and theological readings about Centurions within several accounts in the New Testament. For a quick survey of these sources, Mercer provides readers of Scripture a helpful historical and theological guide to the identity of these military figures."

Shawn J. Wilhite
Associate Professor of New Testament,
California Baptist University

Roman Centurions

Studies in the Ancient Church

Early Christian Creeds & Hymns:
What the Earliest Christians Believed in Word and Song
Tony Costa

The Shameful Act:
Marriage and Sexual Intimacy in Tertullian of Carthage
Hannah Turrill

Roman Centurions:
A Historical Analysis of their Role in the New Testament
Steven A. Mercer

Christ Prays with Us:
Learning to Pray with the Early Church
Coleman M. Ford

Roman Centurions

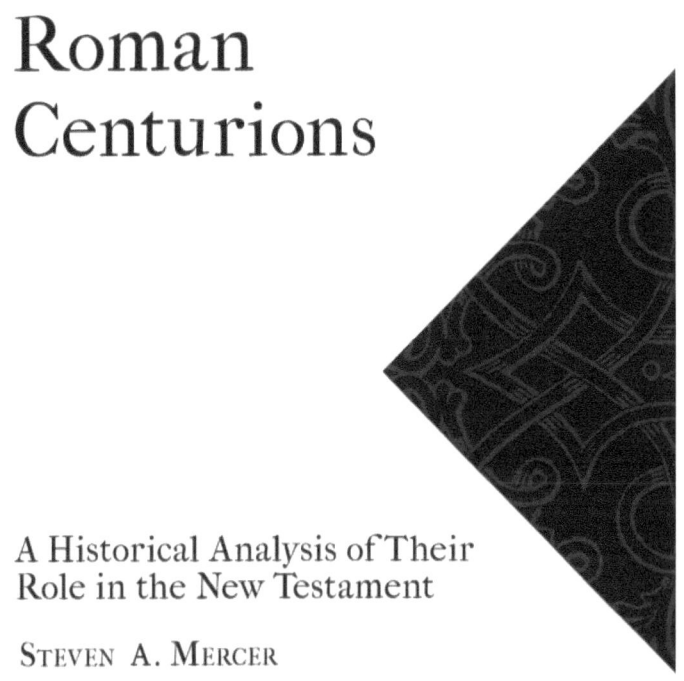

A Historical Analysis of Their
Role in the New Testament

STEVEN A. MERCER

Roman Centurions: A Historical Analysis of Their Role in the New Testament

Series: Studies in the Ancient Church

Copyright © 2023 Steven A. Mercer

All rights reserved. This book may not be reproduced, in whole or in part, without written permission from the publishers.

Unless otherwise indicated, all Scripture quotations are from The ESV® Bible (The Holy Bible, English Standard Version®), copyright © 2001 by Crossway, a publishing ministry of Good News Publishers. Used by permission. All rights reserved.

H&E Academic, Peterborough, Ontario
www.hesedandemet.com

Cover design by Corey M.K. Hughes
Interior font: Equity Text A

Paperback ISBN: 978-1-77484-092-4
eBook ISBN: 978-1-77484-093-1

To Trevor and Dennis Carpenter.

Both modern-day centurions in their own right, who now wait the coming of the new earth with their Lord and Savior in heaven. We miss you terribly and cannot wait to see you again.

Contents

Series Preface xiii

Foreword... xv
Michael A.G. Haykin

Preface... 1

1. An Evaluation of Scholarship 5

2. Roman Centurions: A Background....................................... 21

3. The Roman Centurion At the Cross 39

4. The Roman Centurion Cornelius.. 49

5. The Roman Centurion, His Servant, and Acts...................... 59

Conclusion 67

About the Author 69

Index 71

Scripture Index.. 73

Bibliography 75

Series Preface

Study of the Ancient Church was a common feature of Protestant theological reflection from the Reformation to the close of the long eighteenth century. Many of the Reformers, like John Calvin and Thomas Cranmer, were avid readers of extra-biblical, early Christian literature, as were most of the Puritans. They did not believe that this literature was canonical or on the same level as Holy Scripture, but they rightly recognized that the roots of the Reformed churches of Europe needed to be grounded in elements of Christian orthodoxy from the first five or six centuries of church history. Doctrinal convictions on the Trinity and the Incarnation that had been hammered out in those first centuries, for instance, still very much informed true Christian thinking. Moreover, Protestant claims to catholicity demanded recognition and evidence of continuity with the Ancient Church.

It is in the spirit of those Protestant and Evangelical forbears that these "Studies in the Ancient Church" are being published. Along with Calvin and Cranmer, Ussher and Owen, we recognize that early Christian thought has much to teach us. And in the various studies being published in this series, we listen afresh to those voices from the past, weighing what we hear against Scripture, discerning and cleaving to what is good and profitable for us in this day. These studies cover the entire range of the Ancient Church from the era of the so-called Apostolic Fathers down to the rise of Islam in the seventh century. We also include the occasional monograph on the New Testament texts, not because we consider the literature of that holy text to be on the same level as the literature that followed in the patristic era, but because the world of Roman

Hellenism was a shared cultural context for both the New Testament period and the world of the Ancient Church.

It is the prayer of the publisher that this small academic series may, in its own small way, serve the cause of the Gospel and help advance the glory of God

Foreword

I have long been fascinated by the place of the Roman centurion in the various books of the New Testament. In many ways, these men were the real architects of Roman imperialism and that through their bravery and sometimes brutal disciplining of the ranks of the Roman legions.

Centurions go back into the earliest periods of Roman history and were still a part of the armies of Byzantium in its final days—a span of some two thousand years. They were natural leaders who would stand their ground in each and every battle condition, and were ready to die at their posts. They were the first to charge into battle and had to be the last to quit the field. Centurions were also often employed to execute commando raids, which again speaks of their courage and resourcefulness, and as spokespersons for their commanders, which indicates their leadership abilities.

It is indeed telling that very few of the so-called movers and shakers of what was then the Roman Empire in its heyday appear in the pages of Holy Scripture. Yet, there are a number of centurions. It is noteworthy, for instance, that the first Gentile to be converted was the centurion in charge of the execution of Jesus (see Mark 15:39) and, of course, the conversion of the centurion Cornelius was a turning-point in the history of salvation.

So, I am thrilled that Steven Mercer has taken what originated as a master's thesis and turned it into this small book that examines the Roman centurion, both within the pages of Roman history and also in God's sacred story. It shows how God used some of the unlikeliest of men to further his Kingdom. A must read!

Michael Azad A.G. Haykin
December 20, 2022.

Preface

The Roman centurions in the New Testament were a natural topic to research and write about. Prior to starting the Master of Divinity program at The Southern Baptist Theological Seminary, I served for more than a decade in the United States Army as a Green Beret with the 5th Special Forces Group. The 5th Special Forces Group, nicknamed "The Legion," is one of the most storied military units in the past sixty years. The Legion played an outsized role in the United States war in Vietnam and spearheaded the invasions of both Afghanistan and Iraq after the turn of the millennium.[1] The soldiers of the 5th Special Forces Group seek to follow in the footsteps of Roman legionaries who were the might of the Roman Empire and the most deadly military force of their time. My time with The Legion played a significant part in shaping who I am today and, even though it has been more than seven-years since I left the Army, continues to influence my interest in the military history of Rome. Thus, researching and writing about the Roman centurions mentioned in the New Testament served both my academic as well as my personal interests.

The idea for this particular project began in the Fall of 2018 when I enrolled in a course taught by Dr. Michael Haykin titled *The Early Church in its Greaco-Roman Context*. The course interested me from the outset as, despite majoring in history at the undergraduate level, I knew very little about the vast Roman Empire or the broader cultural context into which Christianity emerged.

---

[1] United States Army Special Operations Command, "5th Special Forces Group (Airborne) History," https://www.soc.mil/USASFC/Groups/5th/5thSFGHistory.html.

1

Yet, this was the culture that formed the background, assumptions, and worldview of each of the writers and subjects in the New Testament. I was fascinated learning about literacy among the Roman population, discovering just how expensive it was for Matthew to write his gospel, and reading about the epicurean philosophers Paul debated. While none of this information changed the truth of the gospel or the theological foundations of my faith, it did open up the pages of the New Testament in a way that I can only describe as seeing things in color for the first time. Learning about life in the early Roman Empire simply added a vibrance and depth that I appreciate more every time I read the scripture. So, when Dr. Haykin asked me if I would be interested in doing further research in this area, I jumped at the chance to write a historical analysis of the Roman centurions in the New Testament.

It is easy to forget that each figure we read about in the New Testament was a living, breathing person with a family, a personality, and a history of their own. I often find that I get so caught up in the main thrust of a story I am reading that the characters become caricatures and serve only to advance the overall plot line. The problem is that this obscures the background and decreases the depth of the story. God uses real, complicated, and three dimentional people to accomplish His work on this earth. These are the same real, complicated, and three dimentional people who Jesus came to save, whom the Holy Spirit indwells, and whom the New Testament authors wrote about. Some of these people are who I will try to introduce to you in the pages that follow and who I pray you will have a greater appreciation for when you have finished reading.

The first chapter reviews the contemporary scholarship of Roman centurions in the New Testament, which has been surprisingly sparse. Other than one failed attempt in the 1930s, no author has really sought to understand who these men were and why they are important enough for the New Testament writers to include in their manuscripts. The second chapter provides an overview of classical and military historical scholarship on Roman centurions and delivers a wealth of information about almost every aspect of these men's lives. Building on this data, chapters 3, 4, and 5 provide as much of a biography of the different individual Roman centurions mentioned in the New Testament as possible. Chapter 3 is devoted to the Roman centurion who crucified Jesus Christ and his role in Matthew, Mark, and Luke's gospels. Chapter 4 highlights the centurion Cornelius, to whom God sent the Apostle Peter to preach a message of faith and repentance. Chapter 5 then looks at the Roman centurion who asked Jesus to heal his servant and covers the other centurions mentioned in the book of Acts. Through these chapters it becomes clear that centurions play more than a minor role in the events of the New Testament and were included by the New Testament writers for a purpose. Understanding who these men were, then helps us to see that purpose more clearly.

I will forever be indebted to the many people who have made this work possible. The men that I served with on ODAs 542 and 516 forever shaped my life and, for better or worse, helped mold me into the man I am today. Of all of these men, Luke V. and Jake T., in their own unique ways, modeled selfless leadership and gave me great examples to strive towards. In addition, Jake and his wife Emily introduced me to proper theology and good biblical teachers. I praise God for our friendship. Dr. Amy Ackerberg-Hastings, who supervised my undergraduate degree in history at the Univeristy of Maryland University College, taught me to be a historian and to be a better writer. While I am still working to improve at both of these tasks, I am better now for her hard work and patient instruction. Dr. Michael A.G. Haykin mentored me as a seminary student and taught me the value of historical scholarship in biblical studies. I cannot imagine a better professor to learn from nor a better example of a Christian historian to attempt to emulate. My friend Trevor Carpenter, to whom this book is partly dedicated, introduced me to Jesus. What better gift can one person give another? And last, but certainly not least, my wife Caroline and our six children (Jonathan, Adeline, Annabelle, James, Audriana, and Jeremiah), whose love and support make waking every morning a blessing and each day a joy to be treasured.

1
An Evaluation of Scholarship

Roman centurions often appear in the New Testament, including at some of the most critical junctures. A Roman centurion led the soldiers who crucified Jesus and exclaimed, "Truly this was the Son of God," after Jesus died.[1] The same centurion praised God and said, "Certainly this man was innocent," according to Luke's crucifixion account, and later may have delivered Jesus' body over to Joseph of Arimathea.[2] In Acts 10, God sent Peter to preach the Gospel to Cornelius, "a centurion of what was known as the Italian Cohort" and "an upright and God-fearing man."[3] Jesus healed the servant of a Roman centurion in Matthew 8 and Luke 7. Multiple centurions were involved in rescuing Paul from being beaten to death in the temple in Jerusalem.[4] A centurion intervened to prevent Paul, a Roman citizen, from being unlawfully whipped, and centurions later organized a guard to protect Paul from being assassinated by the Jews.[5] When Paul was officially put in prison, centurions ran the prison's day-to-day activities, and one of them escorted Paul on his trip to Rome.[6] Finally, the Praetorian Guard ran the prison where Paul was held in Rome.[7] While the New Testament does not directly mention a centurion within the Praetorian Guard, we know that a number of centurions served in that unit and would have most likely interacted with Paul.

---

[1] Matthew 27:54 and Mark 15:39.
[2] Luke 23:47 and Mark 15:44–45.
[3] Acts 10:1–22.
[4] Acts 21:32.
[5] Acts 22:25–26 and 23.
[6] Acts 24 and 27.
[7] Philippians 1:12–13.

Roman Centurions

As centurions played a pivotal role in the events of the New Testament, understanding who these men were proves helpful in understanding the background and context of the related New Testament passages. However, most contemporary scholars have only incidentally investigated the Roman centurions to serve a broader theological or biblical studies argument. For example, in 1987, Glenn N. Davies wrote an article on Cornelius the centurion in Acts 10, but focused entirely on the timeline of Cornelius' salvation and overlooked his profession entirely.[8] In 2002, authors Theodore W. Jennings and Tat-Siong Benny Liew wrote an article on the Roman centurion mentioned in Matthew 8 and argued that the Roman centurion was asking Jesus to heal his adolescent "'boy love' within a pederastic relationship" rather than his servant or son.[9] While Jennings and Liew attempted to place the Roman centurion in his historical context, D.B. Saddington helpfully noted, in his response to Jennings and Liew, that their thesis fails to take into account the nature of the available literary evidence and the complicated military situation in Galilee at the time of the reported event.[10] In 2008, Justin R. Howell wrote an article, building on the work of C. Kavin Rowe, attempting to understand the

---

[8] Glenn N. Davies, "When Was Cornelius Saved?" *The Reformed Theological Review* 46, no. 2 (May 1987): 43–49.

[9] Theodore W. Jennings Jr. & Tat-Siong Benny Liew, "Mistaken Identities but Model Faith: Rereading the Centurion, the Chap and the Christ in Matthew 8:5-13," *Journal of Biblical Literature* 123, no. 3 (September 2004): 468. Jennings and Liew attempt to make their case by arguing that the best understanding for the Greek word παῖς in Matthew 8 is as the "passive member (usually though not necessarily an adolescent boy) of same-sex relationship." Jennings and Liew, "Mistaken Identities but Model Faith," 473.

[10] D.B. Saddington, "The Centurion in Matthew 8:5-13: Considering the Proposal of Theodore W. Jennings Jr., and Tat-Siong Benny Lew," *Journal of Biblical Literature* 125, no. 1 (2006): 140–142. Saddington notes that Jennings and Liew make their case for the definition of the Greek word παῖς based on a classical, rather than koinē, understanding of the word and that the only literary evidence they cite is the word being used to describe rape victims and an adolescent homosexual love interest in a satirical poem by Martial. He also helpfully notes that a centurion in Galilee would have most likely been a part of the Herodian Army and, therefore, may or may not have been Roman himself.

Evaluation of Scholarship

Cornelius narrative in Luke as an explicit critique of the Roman imperial cult of emperor worship.[11] While each of these articles looked at Roman centurions in the New Testament, few authors sought to explicitly understand who the Roman centurions were within their cultural context, and none succeeded.

This is not to suggest, however, that scholarship on Roman centurions during the 1st century AD is lacking. There is, in fact, a cornucopia of useful scholarship discussing every aspect of the lives of Roman soldiers and Roman centurions from recruitment in Spain, on campaign in Britain, to the clothing they wore while off-duty in Jerusalem.[12] However, these works have been conducted by classical and military historians, who utilize the New Testament accounts of Roman centurions to advance their knowledge of Roman centurions in general, rather than utilizing their knowledge of Roman centurions to better understand the centurions of the New Testament in particular. Thus, the current situation is one in which much has been written about Roman centurions in general, but little of that knowledge has been put to use in biblical studies.

Scholarship Specific to Centurions in the New Testament

One of the first attempts to address the Roman centurions in the New Testament from a historical perspective occurred in 1932 when Judson Chastain wrote a PhD dissertation at The Southern Baptist Theological Seminary entitled, "The Roman centurions in the New Testament." Chastain looked first at the role centurions played in the Roman Army as background and then devoted a

---

[11] Justin R. Howell, "The Imperial Authority and Benefaction of Centurions and Acts 10:34–43: A Response to C. Kavin Rowe," *Journal for the Study of the New Testament* 31, no. 1 (September 2008): 25–51.

[12] Works by Dr. Adrian Goldsworthy, Stephen Dando-Collins, and the Elite and Men-at-Arms series by Osprey Press are excellent examples and each of these works will be discussed below in the section on scholarship relating to Roman centurions in general.

chapter to discussing each of the Roman centurions mentioned in the New Testament. He relied heavily on Polybius and Julius Caesar for his primary source material and cited a broad range of secondary sources dating from 1844 to 1931. Chastain argued that Roman centurions served as mid-level military leaders in the Roman infantry, cavalry, artillery, and on the staff of senior military officers.[13] To Chastain, centurions were equivalent to senior Non-Commissioned Officers or a low-level Commissioned Officers in present-day western militaries, whose job it was to command a maneuver element in combat. Chastain wrote that none of the senior military officers "had the very faintest idea of what they were required to teach their soldiers" and that "the only men at all skilled in the profession of arms were the centurions, who were chosen from among the common militia."[14] He also understood the centurions serving in staff positions as both supporting and advising senior officers and the position itself as preparing the centurion for promotion and advancement. Indeed, Chastain argued that the Roman Tribune in Acts 22 had previously served as a centurion and even mentions in passing, "retired centurions who had become senators," as if centurions rising to the senatorial class was common.[15]

Chastain's interpretation of the nature and role of Roman centurions shaped his interpretation of each centurion he discussed from the New Testament. Chastain argued that "the centurions of the palace cohort in Jerusalem doubtless looked on indulgently, but without taking part, as the common soldiers smote and mocked and spat upon our Savior," assuming that type of violence would be beneath the station of a Roman centurion.[16] In the same

---

[13] Judson Chastain, "The Roman Centurion in the New Testament," (PhD diss., The Southern Baptist Theological Seminary, 1932), 1–17.
[14] Chastain, "Roman Centurion in the New Testament," 27–28.
[15] Chastain, "Roman Centurion in the New Testament," 8, 32.
[16] Chastain, "Roman Centurion in the New Testament," 23.

manner, Chastain also argued that no Roman centurion took part in gambling for the possessions of Christ at the crucifixion because this "was all beneath the dignity of a centurion, we may be sure. Officers frequently gamble and joke together, but it is not common to find an officer mingling with his men with so much familiarity."[17]

Chastain also viewed centurions as "the last remnant of a vanishing Roman middle class" that "represented that which was highest and noblest in Roman manhood."[18] He suggested that the Roman centurion who asked Jesus to heal his servant in Matthew 8 and Luke 7 was a model citizen because of Jesus' praise for his faith and held both this centurion and the centurion Cornelius in high regard as men, citizens, and Christians.[19] In other words, these Christian centurions were to be pillars of virtue whom contemporary Christians could model themselves after, but even those who crucified Christ also had some excellent virtue qualities to emulate.

Chastain forced his understanding of the southern United States of the 1930s upon the ancient Roman world and interpreted the evidence accordingly. He believed the United States to be the successor nation to the great and noble Roman Republic. Chastain argued that every great nation must have a middle class as its "backbone," and thus, the Roman Republic must have had a lofty and robust middle class.[20] He then understood the Roman centurion as the embodiment of this middle-class ideal and thus concluded that they held to the same virtues as an idealized noble Christian gentleman in the southern U.S. in the 1930s.[21] This

---

[17] Chastain, "Roman Centurion in the New Testament," 54.
[18] Chastain, "Roman Centurion in the New Testament," 19.
[19] Chastain, "Roman Centurion in the New Testament," 40.
[20] Chastain, "Roman Centurion in the New Testament," 20.
[21] This is specifically suggested in Chastain's assertion of what type of activities Roman Centurions would and would not have participated in, such as casting lots for Jesus' possessions, and the inner dialogues and conversations Chastain supposed the

thought process skewed his understanding and interpretation of the Roman centurions in the New Testament considerably.

Chastain also interpreted the Roman military as being organized in a way that the U.S. Army would have been during the Civil War, with officers serving in infantry, cavalry, artillery, and staff positions without making any distinction between the Imperial and Auxiliary forces in the Roman military. As such, he believed that centurions lived close to where they fought and, if they did travel to fight, they did not live on campaign for extended periods of time.[22] Chastain frequently cited evidence specific to an earlier period in Roman history as supporting his conclusions regarding centurions who lived hundreds of years later.[23] He did correctly understand that the senior military leadership of the Roman Army was comprised of politically-connected appointees, but assumed that these men had no real understanding of military tactics and warfare and argued that all military expertise lay with the centurions. It either slipped his mind that the primary source material he used in writing the dissertation was, in fact, written by senior, politically-connected men who had mastered military tactics and warfare or he believed Julius Caesar, at some point, held the rank of centurion before rising to become Emperor.

More recently, in 2013, Despina Iosif wrote a book attempting to look at early Christian attitudes toward military service. While she did not look at Roman centurions in particular, she did go into great detail in seeking to evaluate as much available primary source material as possible to adequately gauge the general early

---

Roman Centurions of the New Testament to have had, which are frequently found in his dissertation.

[22] Chastain, "Roman Centurion in the New Testament," 7.

[23] For example, on pages 9–11 Chastain uses a speech by the Centurion Spurius Liustinus from 171 BC to draw comparisons to the Centurions of the New Testament time period. On pages 11–12, Chastain also uses Spurius Liustinus' career progression to assume the same career progression for Roman Centurions in the New Testament period without making any distinction between the Roman Army as organized under the Republic and the Imperial Roman Army of the New Testament time period.

EVALUATION OF SCHOLARSHIP

Christian attitudes toward the military and warfare. Iosif's work dealt strictly with the material before Emperor Constantine came to power, including early Christian writings and "a plethora of tombstones that belonged to early Christians in which they, or their nearest and dearest, unequivocally expressed their pride for their having military careers."[24] Her stated goal in writing the book was to "refute the well-established notion that all the early Christians were pacifists" and, interestingly enough, she makes a rather convincing argument even though some of her conclusions about the primary source material are naïve and problematic.[25] Despite its obstacles, however, Iosif's book is important to the study of centurions in the New Testament because it chronicles how early Christians understood the military, interpreted the biblical passages in which centurions are mentioned, and contains an almost exhaustive listing of early Christian primary source material in which the Roman Army is mentioned or discussed.

Most biblical commentaries, by their nature and design, provide little information about the centurions mentioned in the New Testament.[26] The Anchor Bible only mentions that the centurion

---

[24] Despina Iosif, *Early Christian Attitudes to War and Military Service* (Piscataway, NJ: Gorgias Press, 2013), 4. It is important to note that Iosef understands early Christian writing to be everything written by anyone who claimed to be Christian or any writing understood contemporarily to have been Christian in origin. This, of course, includes a number of writings that were rejected by the early Church, the New Testament apocrypha, and other theologically problematic works.

[25] Iosif, *Early Christian Attitudes to War and Military Service*, 11. Iosif does an excellent job of noting early Christian arguments in favor of military service based on the New Testament passages in which Roman Centurions are mentioned but writes in her conclusion that early Christians were "uninterested in the salvation of the soul of individual soldiers" and instead "turned their attention to high-ranking officials in the palace and in the army" (page 305). Her conclusion is based on the understanding that the New Testament books were written in such a way as to defend and endear Christianity to the Roman authorities and is essentially making an argument from silence. However, one could assume that when Paul wrote that the entire Praetorian Guard had heard the Gospel (Phil. 1:12-13), this included individual soldiers.

[26] This brief survey of biblical commentaries is not exhaustive and only includes a few major series. Discussion is limited to the account of Jesus healing the centurion's servant and the centurion Cornelius in Acts 10 because these accounts provide the

in Matthew 8 was most likely a Gentile, but the volume on Luke provides slightly more detail, noting that the centurion was in charge of "a Roman company of one hundred men."[27] Similarly, the Baker Exegetical Commentary volume on Matthew states, "A centurion commanded about a hundred soldiers (a "century") and was subordinate to a tribune."[28] Joel Green, in his commentary on Luke 7, drew a theological comparison between the Roman centurion and the Old Testament military leader Naaman but said little about the Roman centurion's background or profession.[29] The Anchor Bible makes no commentary on the background or role of a centurion while discussing Cornelius in Acts 10, while F.F. Bruce briefly mentioned the role of a centurion in the Roman Army and quoted Polybius regarding the character of centurions in general.[30]

One exception to this trend is Darrell Bock's twin commentaries on Luke and Acts in the Baker Exegetical Commentary on the New Testament series. In his 1994 commentary on Luke, Bock provided a brief synopsis of the centurion pictured in Luke 7, writing that his rank was between that of a chiliarch and a decurion.[31] Bock wrote that the centurion under the command of Herod Antipas had the command of one hundred men, could have been from

---

most information about the individual centurions in question and are thus most likely to contain the most background discussion.

[27] William Foxwell Albright and C. S. Mann, eds., *Matthew*, 1st ed., The Anchor Bible, vol. 26 (Garden City, NY: Doubleday, 1971), 92 and Joseph A. Fitzmyer, *The Gospel According to Luke: Introduction, Translation, and Notes*, 1st. ed., The Anchor Bible, vol 28-28a (Garden City, NY: Doubleday, 1981), 650.

[28] David L. Turner, *Matthew*, Baker Exegetical Commentary on the New Testament (Grand Rapids, MI: Baker Academic, 2008), 232.

[29] Joel B. Green, *The Gospel of Luke*, The New International Commentary on the New Testament (Grand Rapids, MI: W. B. Eerdmans Publishing, 1997), 284.

[30] Joseph A. Fitzmyer, *The Acts of the Apostles*, 1st ed., The Anchor Bible, vol. 31 (Garden City, NY: Doubleday, 1998), 446-469 and F.F. Bruce, *The Book of the Acts*, The New International Commentary on the New Testament (Grand Rapids, MI: W. B. Eerdmans Publishing, 1988), 201-202.

[31] Darrell I. Bock, *Luke*, Baker Exegetical Commentary on the New Testament (Grand Rapids, MI: Baker Books, 1994), 635.

Evaluation of Scholarship

a variety of nationalities, earned a significant amount of money, and that he would have been uneducated and uncultured.[32] The problem with Bock's historical portrait is that it contains a mixture of accurate and inaccurate information.[33] In Bock's 2007 commentary on Acts, he wrote that the centurion Cornelius was "a commander of one of the six units of one hundred men within a cohort" and that he would have served under a tribune.[34] He also included a quotation from Polybius noting that centurions were "good leaders, of steady and prudent mind," but he did not go into further detail about Cornelius' profession.[35]

Scholarship on Roman Centurions in General

In his short book on Roman centurion's between 31 BC and AD 500, author Raffaele D'Amato provided a plethora of detailed information regarding Roman centurions during the period in which the events of the New Testament took place and were chronicled. He noted that Roman centurions were "professional fighting men—sometimes with as much as 20 years' experience under their belt—who maintained day-to-day training, discipline, and organization, and who provided personal tactical leadership in battle."[36] Their general role in the Roman Army was to provide "the crucial level of command between the military tribunes and the common soldiers," although D'Amato helpfully pointed out that there are examples of centurions serving in other roles such as

---

[32] Bock, *Luke*, 635–636.

[33] A Chiliarch is a dated term and refers to the rank of Tribune. A Decurion did not command 10 men but was rather the equivalent rank of the centurion in a Roman cavalry unit. While this centurion very well could have been under the command of Herod Antipas, was certainly paid well, and could have been a variety of nationalities, a general requirement for the rank of centurion was to be literate, thus some level of education and culture would have been common among centurions.

[34] Darrell I. Bock, *Acts*, Baker Exegetical Commentary on the New Testament (Grand Rapids, MI: Baker Academic, 2007), 385.

[35] Bock, *Acts*, 385.

[36] Raffaele D'Amato, *Roman Centurions 31 BC–AD 500: The Classical and Late Empire* (Oxford: Osprey Publishing, 2012), 3.

training officer.³⁷ In addition to their military duties, centurions also oversaw logistical functions for the Empire, performed police duties, escorted prisoners, and even served as judicial authorities in matters involving assaults, thefts, tax collection, and other low-level criminal activities.³⁸

D'Amato offered significant detail regarding the hierarchy within the Roman Centurionate. He explained that the Second through Tenth Cohorts in a typical Roman legion had six centurions, "titled, from junior to senior, as the *hastatus posterior, hastatus prior, princeps posterior, princeps prior, pilus posterior,* and *pilus prior.*³⁹ The First Cohort in the legion, *cohors prima,* "had twice the number of men" and "consisted of five, not six double-sized *centuriae,* commanded by centurions termed collectively as *primi ordines.*"⁴⁰ The centurions of the First Cohort, in ascending order, were titled *"hastatus posterior, princeps posterior, hastatus, princeps,* and *primus pilus."*⁴¹ Thus, the *primus pilus* was the highest ranking centurion and was only outranked by eight other officers in a Roman legion.⁴²

Roman centurions usually began their military service as ordinary soldiers and rose through the ranks, although there are examples of some centurions who were directly commissioned to the position. D'Amato noted that a number of men from the Equestrian class and a few from the Senatorial class were appointed as centurions.⁴³ The criteria that D'Amato suggested

---

³⁷ D'Amato, *Roman Centurions 31 BC–AD 500,* 7.
³⁸ D'Amato, *Roman Centurions 31 BC–AD 500,* 14-15.
³⁹ D'Amato, *Roman Centurions 31 BC–AD 500,* 4.
⁴⁰ D'Amato, *Roman Centurions 31 BC–AD 500,* 4-5.
⁴¹ D'Amato, *Roman Centurions 31 BC–AD 500,* 5.
⁴² D'Amato, *Roman Centurions 31 BC–AD 500,* 5.
⁴³ D'Amato, *Roman Centurions 31 BC–AD 500,* 9 & 17. The appointment of each centurion was approved by the Emperor himself, which provided an opening for well-connected persons to request an appointment for a family member or client. D'Amato suggested that those who were directly commissioned to the office of Centurion either "wished to follow the profession of arms seriously" or were of "straitened financial circumstances" (page 9). He also noted the few examples we have of centurions being

EVALUATION OF SCHOLARSHIP

were used to select centurions included bravery, leadership, stature, strength, skill at arms, vigilance, temperance, a readiness to execute orders without question, being a strict disciplinarian, active in exercising soldiers, at least 30 years old, and literate.[44] However, these qualifications were ideals and not rigidly enforced.[45] D'Amato's book also has sections describing the overall social status of the centurions and their role in religious practices common to the Roman military.

D'Amato went into great detail in describing what Roman centurions would have worn and the military equipment they would have used. During the New Testament period, Roman centurions wore a helmet with a transverse crest and silvered insignia, ring-mail armor with "an appliqué Medusa mask on the breast" or a muscled cuirass of metal or leather, and greaves.[46] They also carried a half-trapezoidal shield called a *scutum*, a gladius sword with a highly decorated scabbard worn on the left side of the body, and the infamous *vitis*, or vine staff, used for disciplining soldiers.[47]

Similarly, Ross Cowan published two short books on the Roman legionary between 58 BC and AD 69 and the Roman legionary from AD 69 to 161. Although neither book adds to the information and detail that D'Amato provides on Roman centurions, each of Cowan's books provide valuable supplemental information to properly understand Roman centurions during the 1st century AD. The study of the Roman legionary between 58 BC and AD 69 is important because, as most Roman centurions were promoted

---

promoted to senior military positions or Senators were directly commissioned as Centurions and were already at least members of the Equestrian class before their military service (page 12). This would suggest that most centurions who rose through the ranks could only hope, at best, to advance to the Equestrian class.

[44] D'Amato, *Roman Centurions 31 BC-AD 500*, 9.

[45] For example, D'Amato notes that the youngest Centurion we know of was just 18 years old when appointed by direct commission (*Roman Centurions 31 BC-AD 500*, 9).

[46] D'Amato, *Roman Centurions 31 BC - AD 500*, 19-33.

[47] D'Amato, *Roman Centurions 31 BC - AD 500*, 21-38.

through the ranks, it is highly likely that the Roman centurions mentioned in the New Testament served as regular legionary soldiers during this period. Thus, Cowan's book provides a portrait of the Roman centurion as he entered military service, learned his craft, and rose through the ranks. It also provides an overview of the type of soldiers under the average Roman centurion's command. Cowan's second book on the Roman legionary from AD 69 to 161 is also helpful because it paints a portrait of the average soldier under a centurion's command during the later New Testament period. The book also helps contemporary scholars understand some of the change that took place in the life of the average soldier throughout the 1st century AD.

Another short book in the same series, written by Boris Rankov, deals explicitly with the Praetorian Guard. While some of the details of Rankov's book contradict that of D'Amato and Cowan, he provided relevant information in helping modern readers understand the structure, function, and duties of the Praetorian Guard itself.[48] For example, Rankov composed a helpful overview of the political power of the senior officers of the Praetorian Guard, including the centurions, and noted the fact that the Julio-Claudian emperors maintained a German bodyguard force that protected the emperor and fought alongside the Praetorian Guard in combat.[49]

A very helpful single volume on understanding Roman centurions is *The Complete Roman Army* by Adrian Goldsworthy. Goldsworthy's book provides a short introduction to Roman history, a chronology of the wars fought by Rome, and then includes

---

[48] For example. Rankov states that equestrians wishing for a direct appointment as a centurion had to give up their equestrian status (page 10), while both D'Amato and Cowan argue otherwise. However, given that Rankov's work was published some 20 years before D'Amato's and Cowan's, as well as that of Adrian Goldsworthy and Stephen Dando-Collins, many of these contradictions can probably be attributed to advances in scholarship over the last 20 years.

[49] Boris Rankov, *The Praetorian Guard* (Oxford: Osprey Publishing, 1994), 10–11.

EVALUATION OF SCHOLARSHIP

a detailed overview of the Roman Army during the Republic. Each of these sections offers excellent background material to assist in understanding the central section of the book, which deals with the Army of the Principate. Goldsworthy detailed the function and role of each level of officer and individual soldier in the Roman Army. He wrote chapters on what it was like to join the Army, the life and daily routine of a soldier, being off-duty, religion in the military, the soldier's duties during peacetime, and three in-depth chapters on how the Army fought in battle.

The level of detail Goldsworthy related on the Roman military is invaluable for studying Roman centurions in general and in studying the Roman centurions mentioned in the New Testament in particular. For example, like many other authors, Goldsworthy noted that Roman soldiers were forbidden to marry.[50] However, he also noted that "the ban on marriage did not apply to senior officers from the senatorial and equestrian classes, nor to legionary centurions, and probably not to auxiliary centurions."[51] He went on to write that "Senatorial and equestrian officers were expressly forbidden to marry women from the provinces in which they served, but the same did not apply to centurions, many of whom married locals."[52] While this does not prove the marital status of any centurion mentioned in the New Testament, this bit of detail does argue against Jennings and Liew's proposal that the servant in Matthew 8 was the "boy love" of his Roman centurion master and also brings into question the nature of Cornelius' family as well.[53]

---

[50] Adrian Goldsworthy, *The Complete Roman Army* (London: Thames and Hudson, 2011), 102.

[51] Goldsworthy, *The Complete Roman Army*, 103.

[52] Goldsworthy, *The Complete Roman Army*, 104.

[53] Jennings & Liew, "Mistaken Identities but Model Faith," 468. Jennings and Liew specifically argued that, although the Greek word παῖς could mean son, it didn't in this context because Roman soldiers were forbidden to marry, 470.

Goldsworthy also provided details on Roman military retirement. He noted that "a good number of men live near their old base" and "since soldiers often married local women, this acted as another incentive to remain in the province where they had served."[54] "Army veterans also had some privileges, for instance, exemption from certain types of punishment and restrictions on their liability for public service in the local communities, and were also Roman citizens." [55] When Goldworthy's information on military retirement is understood together with D'Amato's estimates that the lowest ranking centurions were paid 15 times that of an average legionary soldier, it is easy to see how Roman centurions could have the financial means to build a synagogue for the Jews and own large family estates.[56]

Another important work by Goldsworthy deals specifically with the Roman Army at war. This book attempts to look at the Roman army as it actually conducted warfare, rather than the ideals portrayed in military manuals.[57] This book is of primary importance because, whatever other tasks the Roman centurion had, his main expertise was in conducting warfare and training his soldiers in military tactics and weaponry. Thus, each Roman centurion would first and foremost have been an expert at fighting and killing. Goldsworthy also provided great insight into the role of the centurion in battle, which was to lead and inspire his men to overcome their natural fear and fight the enemy. He also provided historical examples of centurions inspiring their men, sometimes at the cost of their lives.[58]

---

[54] Goldsworthy, *The Complete Roman Army*, 115.

[55] Goldsworthy, *The Complete Roman Army*, 115.

[56] D'Amato, *Roman Centurions*, 15-16. D'Amato also notes that the highest ranking centurions could have been paid as much as 60 times more than the average Legionary.

[57] Adrian Goldsworthy, *The Roman Army at War 100 BC–AD 200* (Oxford: Clarendon Press, 1998), 10.

[58] Goldsworthy, *The Roman Army at War*, 257-258.

Evaluation of Scholarship

In his seminal book, *Legions of Rome*, Stephen Dando-Collins began by providing a concise overview of the Roman military and the life, equipment, living conditions, and duties of Roman soldiers. His brief section on Roman centurions is insightful and notes a few pieces of information not available in other works. For example, "one centurion typically served with twelve different legions" throughout his career and that the oldest known centurion was 70 years old when he died, still serving after forty-five years with the 3rd Augusta Legion in Africa.[59] The real strength of the book, however, is that it concisely chronicles the unit history of every Imperial Roman Legion as well as the history of many of the major known battles. This section includes information about where the legion served, where it recruited its soldiers, the battles the legion fought in, and information on notable commanders. For instance, the 3rd Gallica Legion was stationed in Judea sometime after 30 AD until being moved to "Moesia, on the Danube, where it arrived in AD 68" after suffering heavy losses in the Jewish Revolt in AD 66.[60] Thus the 3rd Gallica Legion would have been stationed in Judea while the early Christian church was first establishing itself.

Scholarship on Centurions in the Herodian Army

The history of the Herodian Army is another area of scholarship that could provide some background information on centurions in the New Testament. In his excellent work on the army of Herod the Great, Israel Shatzman estimated that Herod's standing army consisted of 16,000 troops, most of them Jews.[61] Further, Herod settled both active and retired military forces in Galilee and

---

[59] Stephen Dando-Collins, *Legions of Rome: The Definitive History of Every Imperial Roman Legion* (New York: Thomas Dunne Books, 2012), 41.

[60] Dando-Collins, *Legions of Rome*, 123.

[61] Israel Shatzman, *The Armies of the Hasmonaeans and Herod: From Hellenistic to Roman Frameworks* (Heidelberg: Mohr Siebeck, 1991), 186–188.

maintained a standing element of his army in Jerusalem.[62] Evidence also suggests that Herod's army was organized and equipped after the manner of the Roman legions as Herod "received command of Roman troops" as early as 43 BC and "a part of the Herodian army was eventually incorporated into the Roman *auxilia*."[63] Even though Herod the Great was dead before Jesus began his ministry, information about his army poses several questions relating to the centurions mentioned in the New Testament. Could any of the centurions mentioned in the New Testament have been Jewish? Does "centurion" automatically refer to Roman soldiers, or were some of the centurions with whom Paul dealt part of the Herodian or former Herodian army? If some of the soldiers who rescued Paul from the Jews, protected him, and traveled with him were Jewish, could the attitude of the Judean Jewish population toward Jews serving in the military have contributed to the soldier's willingness to protect Paul?

Conclusion

A substantial amount of historical and classical scholarship exists on Roman centurions, and significant advancements have been made within the last twenty years. However, biblical scholars have tended to either ignore current historical scholarship or utilize dated material cited from other biblical scholars. This has led to a misleading portrait of the centurion in the New Testament. There is a need for an updated look at the Roman centurions in the New Testament to understand who they were, in general, and as individuals. This study will provide significant background information for New Testament scholars and pastors to aid in exegesis and exposition of the biblical texts.

---

[62] Shatzman, *The Armies of the Hasmonaeans and Herod*, 191–195.
[63] Shatzman, *The Armies of the Hasmonaeans and Herod*, 198–205. See also pages 211 through 216.

2
ROMAN CENTURIONS: A BACKGROUND

Roman centurions were an integral part of the Roman army and the larger Roman society. Roman centurions enjoyed an elite status within the broader Roman citizenry and were a significant part of the first line of interaction between the government and the people living in the Empire. While the centurion was primarily a military rank, it was from this rank that the Roman Empire drew many of its police commanders, magistrates, jailers, and civil administrators. Thus, centurions were not only called upon to be the backbone of the Roman military but also served as the backbone of the Roman government's administrative function.

Military Service

The Roman infantry was organized into different combat units called legions, which were comprised of 10 cohorts, which were made up of six *centuriae*.[1] Each *centuria* had a strength of 80 men and was commanded by a centurion.[2] The first cohort in each legion was twice as large as the others and was composed of those selected as the best soldiers in the legion.[3] Thus, the strength of the average cohort was 480 men (960 for the first cohort), which

---

[1] Goldsworthy, *Roman Army at War*, 13.
[2] Goldsworthy, *Roman Army at War*, 13.
[3] Flavius Vegetius Renatus, *De Re Militari* (Concerning Military Affairs): The Classic Treatise on Warfare at the Pinnacle of the Roman Empire's Power (United Kingdom: Leonaur, 2012) 42; Goldsworthy, *The Roman Army at War*, 13-14. Although Vegetius wrote *De Re Militari* in the 5th century, he states in his preface to the third book that the emperor had ordered Vegetius to create an abridged work compiling military "maxims and instructions" of the ancients. In other words, Vegetius' work was focused on the Roman military during the republic and the early empire, thus making this 5th century work flawed, but helpful in some aspects to this study.

put a legion at around 5,280 soldiers. Of this group, 66 men would have been centurions.[4]

Almost all centurions started out as Roman legionary soldiers and the soldiers were recruited heavily from modern-day Italy until the mid-1st century.[5] Roman citizenship was required to join the army, but most recruits came from poorer economic classes.[6] These men would have been attracted to voluntary military service because the army provided regular pay, medical care, clothing, food, and a grant of land or a large monetary sum upon retirement.[7] The major downside to army service was the 25-year enlistment and the reality that one might not live to receive the promised retirement benefits. No more than 45% completed the full 25 years.[8] However, if a man had some level of education, a successful army career could provide the attention and necessary connections required for social advancement, and the first step in that advancement was to become a centurion.[9]

Centurions were crucial to the success of the Roman military. D'Amato notes that "it was these professional fighting men—sometimes with as much as 20 years' experience under their belt—who maintained day-to-day training, discipline and organization, and who provided personal tactical leadership in battle."[10] The officer corps of the Roman army was largely comprised of political appointees and Roman citizens of the senatorial class. While

---

[4] These numbers are based on Roman military doctrine and would almost certainly have been smaller in practice due to factors including the lack of new recruits, soldiers being called away on temporary duty, soldiers who had run away, soldiers on authorized leave, and soldiers who were sick. Thus these numbers represent the Roman ideal and are probably within a 10-15% margin of actual unit strength. However, key leadership positions would generally have remained filled so the number of centurions would remain fairly stable.

[5] D'Amato, *Roman Centurions*, 6; Cowan, *Roman Legionary*, 11.

[6] Goldsworthy, *The Roman Army at War*, 76–77.

[7] Goldsworthy, *The Roman Army at War*, 77.

[8] Goldsworthy, *The Roman Army at War*, 77; Cowan, *Roman Legionary*, 12.

[9] Goldsworthy, *The Roman Army at War*, 77.

[10] D'Amato, *Roman Centurions*, 3.

these men had a great deal of knowledge regarding tactics, warfare, and the military in general, they dealt with strategic decisions and not the everyday tactical ones. Thus, it was the Roman centurions who bridged the gap between the strategic and the tactical; between the commanders and the common soldiers.[11]

This means that the Roman centurions had to be both an experienced soldier and trusted by their commanders and the men they led. Centurions were required to have proved themselves as brave, capable leaders in battle.[12] They also had to have certain physical qualities, including "stature, strength, and skill at arms."[13] In addition, centurions had to be at least 30 years old and literate.[14] While there were some centurions appointed to or promoted to that rank before reaching 30, there is no evidence that any centurion was unable to read and write, and although there are records of some equestrians being promoted directly to the rank of centurion, this seems to be an exception rather than the rule.[15]

Training Military Soldiers

The primary job of the centurion was to command troops at the tactical level in combat, and the survival of the centurion depended largely on how well he trained his soldiers. During initial training, recruits would learn to handle various weapons—including the sword and shield, spears, slings, bows, and various forms of artillery—as well as swimming and horseback riding.[16] Once weapons were mastered, recruits would then learn tactics, and eventually, mock battles would be fought with "practice weapons

---

[11] D'Amato, *Roman Centurions*, 3.
[12] D'Amato, *Roman Centurions*, 9.
[13] D'Amato, *Roman Centurions*, 9.
[14] D'Amato, *Roman Centurions*, 9.
[15] D'Amato, *Roman Centurions*, 9; Cowan, *Roman Legionary*, 12.
[16] Goldsworthy, *Complete Roman Army*, 81.

or real weapons with their points covered with leather discs to prevent serious injuries."[17] Recruits would begin by fighting each other and progress to mock battles as a part of a unit.[18] All of this training probably lasted several months and was all conducted under the supervision, instruction, and admonishment of a centurion.[19]

Training did not stop once the recruit became a soldier and became a part of an army unit, but was, in fact, a part of everyday life. Josephus wrote of the Roman Army,

> They do not sit with folded hands in peace time only to put them in motion in the hour of need. On the contrary, as though they had been born with weapons in hand, they never have a truce from training, never wait for emergencies to arise. Moreover, their peace maneuvers are no less strenuous than veritable warfare; each soldier daily throws all his energy into his drill, as though he were in action ... Indeed, it would not be wrong to describe their maneuvers as bloodless combats and their combats as sanguinary maneuvers.[20]

So we see that the job of training soldiers did not stop for the centurion and was rather a constant and daily task.

Commanding Combat Troops

All of the day-to-day training and other tasks performed by the centurions had one larger purpose; to be able to field a cohesive, fighting force on the field of combat. At its most basic level, the Roman army relied on infantry formations during combat, and one

---

[17] Goldsworthy, *Complete Roman Army*, 81.
[18] Goldsworthy, *Complete Roman Army*, 81.
[19] Goldsworthy, *Complete Roman Army*, 80-81.
[20] Josephus, *The Jewish War: Books 1-7*, ed. Jeffrey Henderson et al., trans. H. St. J. Thackeray, vol. 2, Loeb Classical Library (Cambridge, MA: Harvard University Press, 1927-1928), 27.

Background

of the primary duties of a *centuria's* centurion was to keep the soldiers in formation.[21] Goldsworthy notes, "Greek military theorists thought it best to place the bravest men in a phalanx in its front and rear ranks. Those in front kept the formation advancing, and actually fought. Those in the rear stopped the others from fleeing."[22] Centurions expected to lead from the front and thus usually formed in the front or right front of the *centuria's* formation so the rest of the men could take direction from him, while other officers formed up in the rear of the cohort to keep things moving along.[23] This is why centurions had an exceptionally high casualty rate.[24]

Roman centurions were frequently cited as performing heroic actions in combat, setting a good example for their fellow soldiers, and being examples for other soldiers to emulate.[25] Caesar wrote of several centurions who performed heroic deeds under his command in various wars. In one narrative, Caesar first cited the fallen heroes of the battle, which included mentioning that centurions were among the fallen.[26] He then noted that many centurions were among the wounded, with "four centurions from one cohort" having "lost an eye."[27] Finally, Caesar noted that the centurion Scaeva was rewarded for bravery, as was the rest of his cohort.[28] This written account served as more than just a historical record, however. One purpose for including this information in his book was that it allowed Caesar to highlight his generosity to those who performed well in combat. Second, the fact that this centurion was named by

---

[21] Goldsworthy, *The Roman Army at War*, 178-182.
[22] Goldsworthy, *The Roman Army at War*, 178.
[23] Goldsworthy, *The Roman Army at War*, 182.
[24] Goldsworthy, *The Roman Army at War*, 182.
[25] Goldsworthy, *Complete Roman Army*, 49.
[26] Caesar, *Civil War*, edited and translated by Cynthia Damon, Loeb Classical Library 39 (Cambridge, MA: Harvard University Press, 2016), 270-271.
[27] Caesar, *Civil War*, 270-271.
[28] Caesar, *Civil War*, 270-271.

Roman Centurions

Caesar in his book, including the account of the reward Scaeva received, was sure to be noticed by other centurions and told to other soldiers.[29] In other words, this account told each centurion what was expected of them and provided each soldier with a role model for gallant military service.[30] Thus, centurions were not only examples of leadership in their individual cohorts but were also propped up as examples of heroism in combat.

A Roman centurion's status as the senior and most experienced soldier in the cohort would have automatically given him a certain prestige. Junior soldiers would look to the centurion to provide guidance and to set an example of what it meant to be a Roman soldier. While centurions were supposed to serve as disciplinarians, the ideal centurion was also a protector of the soldiers under his command. Julius Caesar penned a fine example of this ideal in a story about a centurion named Marcus Petronius.

> Marcus Petronius, a centurion of the same legion, had tried to cut down a gate, but was overpowered by superior numbers and in desperate case. Already he had received many wounds, and he cried to the men of his company who had followed him: "As I cannot save myself with you, I will at any rate provide for your life, whom in the eager desire for glory I have brought into danger. When the chance is given do you look after yourselves." With this he burst into the midst of the enemy, and by slaying two shifted the rest a little from the

---

[29] Although centurions were required to be literate, it is doubtful that the average centurion would have been able to afford a copy of Caesar's *Civil War*. However, some centurions would have been able to afford such a luxury and most certainly others would have heard oral accounts of these battle stories from other officers or centurions. It is also probable that military commanders, who were almost exclusively made up of wealthy Roman citizens, would have had small personal libraries. Thus, although it is not certain, it is probably the case that most Roman centurions were familiar with the famous battle stories recounted by Caesar and others; most especially the famous battle stories in which centurions were the heroes.

[30] The same thing occurs in contemporary militaries across the globe and in other militaries throughout history. Accounts of gallantry are told and retold to soldiers in order that these accounts would set an example for other soldiers to follow in combat.

gate. When his men tried to assist him he said: "In vain do you try to rescue my life, for blood and strength are already failing me. Wherefore depart while you have a chance and get you back to the legion." So, a moment later, he fell fighting and saved his men.[31]

Caesar portrays the centurion Marcus Petronius as self-sacrificially protecting his men and caring for their well-being, even as he led them into combat. Thus, the picture of a centurion being a figure of authority and rigid discipline is contrasted in accounts such as this one, in which the centurions are willing to lay down their lives for the protection of their fellow soldiers.

Administrative roles

In addition to their combat duties, centurions also served in various military administrative roles in the Roman army. Under Caesar Augustus, the legion only had two military officers from senatorial rank; the *legatus legionis* and the *tribunus laticlavius*.[32] However, a third officer, the *praefectus castrorum* was a former chief centurion and was in charge of camp administration, particularly any administrative duties that required technical military knowledge.[33] After Augustus, the position of *praefectus castrorum* was open to any member of the equestrian class, however, as it was normal for centurion who reached *primus pilus* to become an equestrian, the position would most often have been filled by promoted centurions.[34] Thus, it stands to reason that centurions had a major role to play in the administration of a Roman military garrison.

---

[31] Caesar, *The Gallic War*, translated by H. J. Edwards, Loeb Classical Library 72 (Cambridge, MA: Harvard University Press, 1917), 452-453.
[32] Goldsworthy, *Complete Roman Army*, 50.
[33] Goldsworthy, *Complete Roman Army*, 50.
[34] Goldsworthy, *Complete Roman Army*, 65.

Roman military camps were arranged in a very particular and regular order all throughout the Roman world. Every legionary fortress had an area set aside for cohort barracks along the outer walls of the rectangular garrison, and each centurion had a private room at the end of their *centuria's* barracks building.[35] The *Principia*, or headquarters building, was located in the center of the camp with the barracks of the first cohort to one side.[36] The *Praetorium*, stables, bathhouses, hospital building, tribune's residences, workshop, and granary also had set locations within the middle of the garrison.[37] A series of walls and fortifications surrounded the entire garrison with only one gate located toward the middle of each section of the four wall sections.[38] Each garrison was built by the Roman soldiers themselves and continued to be improved as that particular Legion was located in that garrison.

This legionary fortress setup required the entire legion to run the administrative activities that were required to support such a large group of people. When not drilling for combat, soldiers found themselves detailed to various duty rosters that could include guarding the gates or walls of the camp, running errands for commanders, conducting patrols outside of the camp, cleaning the bathhouses, and repairing boots for their fellow soldiers.[39] There were too many daily tasks to have all been led by a centurion, but the evidence does show that individual soldiers were assigned to temporary duty under the supervision of the centurions from other cohorts.[40] Several receipts even show that money for legionary soldiers was deposited and held with centurions for later

---

[35] Goldsworthy, *Complete Roman Army*, 82–86.
[36] Goldsworthy, *Complete Roman Army*, 83.
[37] Goldsworthy, *Complete Roman Army*, 83.
[38] Goldsworthy, *Complete Roman Army*, 89.
[39] Goldsworthy, *Complete Roman Army*, 90.
[40] Goldsworthy, *Complete Roman Army*, 90–91.

distribution.⁴¹ This all strongly suggests that it was the centurions who would be charged with the day-to-day administration of these various tasks of running the camp and would direct the soldiers under their command in their accomplishment.

Non-Military Service

In addition to their military service, centurions also served the Roman Empire in civil or political-administrative and other non-military roles. Whether chosen because of their administrative abilities or because of distinguishing themselves in a particular military campaign, centurions were routinely called upon by senior Roman administrators to fill positions and fulfill duties for individuals and the Empire. As noted earlier, Julius Caesar remembered and wrote with fondness of centurions under his command, and it was rather common for senior centurions to be promoted to the Equestrian Order.⁴² It is highly likely then that centurions who found favor with the rising stars among the senatorial class would have found patrons among the same and thus been in a position to receive postings to civil administrative positions both during and after military service.

Police and Magistrates

Active military centurions could be given the rank of *centuriones frumentarii* (or *frumentariorum*), which was the command position over the *frumentarii* soldiers.⁴³ The *frumentarii* soldiers served as an "imperial police and intelligence corps" away from the main legion and reported directly to *castra peregrina*, which was the

---

⁴¹ *Select Papyri, Volume II: Public Documents*, trans. A. S. Hunt & C. C. Edgar, Loeb Classical Library (Cambridge, MA: Harvard University Press, 1934), 465–466.
⁴² Caesar, *Civil War*, 270–271; Caesar, *The Gallic War*, 452–453; Goldsworthy, *Complete Roman Army*, 65.
⁴³ D'Amato, *Roman Centurions*, 7.

headquarters for the police force in Rome.[44] Command of the *frumentarii* units would allow a centurion to operate on his own, away from the main military headquarters, and most likely serve and interact with civilian Roman leadership, who mostly came from the senatorial class. As such, centurions promoted to these positions had to be highly trusted, and excellent service was sure to provide future promotion and advancement.[45]

While serving in this capacity, centurions and the soldiers under them were expected to resolve any number of disputes normally handled by contemporary police forces and judicial services. For example, a man named Syrus Petekas, son of Syrion, wrote to the centurion Ammonius Paternus to complain that two tax collectors, their assistant, and their scribe had assaulted Syrus' mother during a house visit.[46] The amanuensis who wrote the letter, as Syrus was himself illiterate, noted that Syrus had already paid all of the taxes that were due and was writing to the centurion Paternus "that I may obtain justice at your hands."[47] Here the centurion was to resolve two complaints in deciding if Syrus had indeed paid all of the taxes that were owed and if the tax collectors were guilty of assaulting an elderly woman. While it is unclear in the letter if Syrus is indeed asking for the centurion Paternus to act as a judge or arbiter in the case, he is clearly requesting that the centurion act in a police capacity at minimum to assist in bringing the tax collectors to justice.

Another example is provided in a letter that was written to the centurion Aurelius Marcianus. It seems a man named Aurelius Sarapion, son of Pasei, of the village of Philadelphia, wrote that he

---

[44] D'Amato, *Roman Centurions*, 7.
[45] D'Amato, *Roman Centurions*, 7.
[46] Hunt & Edgar, *Select Papyri, Volume II: Public Documents*, 276–277
[47] Hunt & Edgar, *Select Papyri, Volume II: Public Documents*, 276–277

was mistreated at the hands of a soldier named Julius and is looking for the centurion to intervene on his behalf and punish the offending soldier.

> To Aurelius Marcianus, centurion, from Aurelius Sarapion son of Pasei, of the village of Philadelphia. There is nothing more dreadful or harder to bear than maltreatment. At the time of life which I have reached, being eighty years old and more, I am serving blamelessly as an Arab archer. A sow having escaped from my daughter in the village and being reported to be at the house of the soldier Julius, I went to him to demand his oath about this matter, and he laying hands on me, old as I am, in the village in the middle of the day, as if there were no laws, belaboured me with blows in the presence of Nepotianus, steward of the most eminent Valerius Titanianus, and of Maurus and Ammonius, Arab archers, so that they, being shocked to see me beaten, separated us and I barely overcame his attempt on my life. I am compelled to present this petition and to request that he be arrested in order that his audacious behaviour may receive punishment; and I hold him to account. Farewell. (Identification) Sarapion, aged about 84 years, with a scar on the right knee. (Dated) The 6th year of the Emperors and Caesars Marci Julii Philippi Pii Felices Augusti, Hathur 26.[48]

While it is unclear if the centurion Aurelius Marcianus was serving as a legionary centurion or as a *centuriones frumentarii*, what is clear is that the author Sarapion is looking to the centurion to act in an official police capacity to judge a simple assault case and bring the perpetrator to justice. In this instance, it also seems clear that the author is looking to the centurion to act in both a judicial and law enforcement capacity, probably indicating that the centurion has some sort of command authority over the accused soldier.

---

[48] Hunt & Edgar, *Select Papyri, Volume II: Public Documents*, 288–291.

Roman Centurions

People throughout the Roman Empire also wrote to centurions to notify them of suspected crimes. Aurelia Tisais of the village of Tebtunis wrote to the centurion Aurelius Julius Marcellinus to inform him that Tisais' father was missing and presumed murdered.[49] In this case, the centurion is being asked to play detective and solve the murder of Tisais' father, or at least to direct the investigation. Philo wrote of a centurion named Castus, who was tasked with raiding the houses of Jews suspected of hiding weapons.[50] Castus thus would have been confiscating weapons and conducting search and seizure type activities. In both cases, these letters indicate that what the contemporary western world understands to be police matters were handled by centurions and their soldiers in the 1st-century Roman Empire.

While several of the existing letters previously cited show that it could be argued that centurions took on the role of police officers and judges to a certain extent, a letter exists from a group of men of the village of Socnopaei Nesus that was written to the centurion Julius Julianus and specifically asks him to act in a judicial capacity.

> To Julius Julianus, centurion, from Herieus son of Stotoetis, stone-cutter, Paboukas son of Pabous, Herieus son of Pakusis, Apunchis son of Horion, Esouris son of Paouites, Demas son of Demas, Orsenouphis son of Herieus, Petesouchus son of Sotas, Horus whose mother is Thaisas, Soterichus whose father's name is unknown and whose mother is Thaesis, Teikas son of Pakusis, Pates son of Satabous, Pabous son of Pabous, Kannis son of Pates, Sostus son of Pabous, Pais son of Satabous, Pakusis son of Psenesis, Apunchis son of Apunchis, Abous son of Satabous, Pakusis son of Herieus, Pousi

---

[49] Hunt & Edgar, *Select Papyri, Volume II: Public Documents*, 384–387.

[50] Philo. *Every Good Man is Free. On the Contemplative Life. On the Eternity of the World. Against Flaccus. Apology for the Jews. On Providence*, Translated by F.H. Colson, Loeb Classical Library 363 (Cambridge, MA: Harvard University Press, 1941), 348–351.

BACKGROUND

son of Matais, Pakusis son of Apunchis, Satabous son of Pakusis, Aeis son of Kannes, Melas son of Areus, all of the village of Socnopaei Nesus in the division of Heraclides. We submit to you, my lord, a complaint which craves for redress at your hands, the matter being as follows. There exists here a stretch of shore registered as part of the area of our village, consisting of a great number of arurae, and whenever the said land is uncovered by the water, it is leased and sown according to custom, paying rent arura by arura, which rent is delivered in kind to the most sacred Treasury; and it is owing to just this portion of land that all the liabilities of the village, which are very large, are paid, because the village has no private land or Crown land or any other kind. But in order that all may be able to remain in their own homes, especially as the most illustrious praefect Subatianus Aquila has ordered all persons who are strangers to return home and apply themselves to their customary business, we accordingly, seeing that a certain Orseus son of Stotoetis and his brothers, numbering five persons in all, have descended upon us preventing us from sowing the land described, are forced to present this petition, requesting you, if it please you, to order them to be brought before you to answer for their action. Farewell. Year 16, Phaophi 14.[51]

Here the men are looking to the centurion Julius Julianus specifically to settle a land dispute and to order that Orseus and his brothers be brought before him in a manner wholly consistent with a contemporary judicial office. In addition, James Jeffers noted that the primary purpose of the Roman administration in a province was to "maintain the imperial system" and that the senior officials had a "very limited interest ... in local affairs, which did not threaten the stability of the society."[52] As such, it would have largely fallen to

---

[51] Hunt & Edgar, *Select Papyri, Volume II: Public Documents*, 282–285.
[52] James S. Jeffers, *The Greco-Roman World of the New Testament Era: Exploring the Background of Early Christianity* (Downers Grove, IL: IVP Academic, 1999), 114–115.

the centurions to judge these types of minor disputes and forward matters of greater importance to their superiors.

Jailers and Prison guards

Throughout the New Testament, centurions are mentioned as prominent members of the Roman penal system. In Acts 22, it was a Roman centurion who was overseeing the interrogation and flogging of Paul, only to intervene to the Tribune on Paul's behalf when he learned that Paul was a Roman citizen.[53] Throughout Paul's imprisonment, centurions are charged with overseeing his guard force as well as his care.[54] Finally, in Acts 27, a centurion was charged with escorting Paul and some other prisoners to Rome.[55] However, extra-biblical sources also note that Roman centurions were charged with guarding prisoners and the overall administration of the jails under their care.

In Livy's *History of Rome* the Roman historian recounts the story of the wife of a Gallic chieftain named Ortiago, who was captured by the Roman army. She was put in the care of a centurion who raped her and then negotiated to sell her back to her people, only to be murdered in the process.[56] While not the main point of the story, Livy's recounting of the episode provides an account of a Roman centurion being charged as the jailer for at least one captive and his mistreatment of her during this time. It is remarkable to note that Livy writes: "Charged with guarding her was a centurion with a soldier's sexual appetite and greed," suggesting that this was probably not an isolated incident and the mistreatment of

---

[53] Acts 22:24–29.

[54] In Acts 23, Paul asks the centurion in charge of his guard force to take an informant to the Tribune. Also in Acts 23, the Tribune assigned two centurions to command a large guard force to escort Paul safely to the governor Felix. While with Felix, Paul was kept in custody under the charge of a centurion as noted in Acts 24.

[55] Acts 27: 1–43.

[56] Livy, *History of Rom Volume XI: Books 38-40*, ed. and trans. by J.C. Yardley, Loeb Classical Library (Cambridge, MA: Harvard University Press, 2018), 80–83.

BACKGROUND

prisoners—particularly female prisoners—under the care of centurions was probably widespread and routine.

Political Administrators

Centurions could also be promoted to govern equestrian provinces. As noted earlier, centurions were routinely promoted to the equestrian order and to the rank of *praefectus castrorum*, or camp prefect, in a Roman legion.[57] Similarly, the title of prefect was used for equestrian governors until the title was changed to procurator at some point before the middle of the 1st Century AD.[58] The New Testament consistently uses variants of ἡγεμών when referring to Pilate or other governors, but a damaged inscription found in Caesarea Maritima gives Pilate the title of *praefectus*, consistent with an equestrian governorship.[59] While this is not conclusive evidence that Pilate had been a centurion prior to governing Judea, it is not unlikely that this was the case, especially if Pilate had been a centurion under Tiberius when the later served as a military commander. It is also not that far of a stretch to suggest that if a centurion could be promoted to govern an imperial province, former centurions would certainly have been promoted by Roman and local authorities within their provinces for other administrative positions, especially in Judea.

---

[57] Goldsworthy, *Complete Roman Army*, 65.
[58] Goldsworthy, *Complete Roman Army*, 65.
[59] For the references in the New Testament regarding Pilate see Matthew 27:2, 11, 14, 15, 21, 27, 28:14 and Luke 3:1 and 20:20. Variants on ἡγεμών are also used to describe governors in general (Matt. 10:18, Mark 13:9, and 1 Pet. 2:14) and other specific governors such as Felix (Acts 23:24, 26, 33, 24:1, 10) and Festus (Acts 26:30). Interestingly, each time the New Testament mentions the governor's palace it is referred to as the πραιτώριον which was also the title given to the tent of a *praetor* in a Roman military encampment; see William Arndt et al., *A Greek-English Lexicon of the New Testament and Other Early Christian Literature* (Chicago: University of Chicago Press, 2000), 859. Pilate being a former centurion in Tiberius' Army also puts into context some of Pilate's actions while governing Judea such as setting up golden shields with his and Tiberius' names on the walls of Herod's palace. Some of these and his other actions are described in Josephus, *Jewish War 2* and *Jewish Antiquities 18* and are summarized in Jeffers, *Greco-Roman World*, 130–131.

Roman Centurions

It is known that centurions were the only class of military officer who were allowed to marry local women, and many of them did.[60] Further, Roman policy toward governing non-imperial provinces was one that favored Hellenization and rule by co-opting local leadership.[61] These facts combined would have given incentive for some local governments to appoint a former centurion who had married a local woman to a governmental position in an attempt to curry favor with more senior Roman officials. In addition, former centurions who had married local women would have been the ideal candidates for Roman officials to appoint to various local bureaucratic positions as a way to influence and keep tabs on the local leadership. Given that a large number of Roman legions had been stationed in Judea for some time, it seems likely that several local administrative positions would have been filled by former centurions.

Conclusion

While this chapter has only provided a brief overview of the life and duties of Roman centurions, it is this background that will help bring to light the life of the specific Roman centurions mentioned in the New Testament and their contributions to the text. At the same time, this is not necessarily meant to be an exhaustive study on Roman centurions, and much more information is available.[62] While some new information will be discussed in the coming chapters, it is important to note that the basis of this study is

---

[60] Goldsworthy, *Complete Roman Army*, 103-104.
[61] Jeffers, *Greco-Roman World*, 110-120.
[62] Adriane Goldsworthy's book *The Complete Roman Army* is a great starting point on the study of the Roman military in general and is chalk full of information on Roman centurions in particular. Raffaele D'Amato provides a short but illuminating study on centurions in his book *Roman Centurions 31 BC-AD 500: The Classical and Late Empire*. In addition, I highly recommend James S. Jeffers book *The Greco-Roman World of the New Testament Era: Exploring the Background of Early Christianity* as supplemental reading to help put the information about Roman centurions into a cultural and political context. Finally, to understand a bit of what the Roman centurions thought about

the assumption that the centurions mentioned in the New Testament are included for a specific reason. It is not by accident that God ordained that his Word would mention that Cornelius was a centurion or that it would include a phrase uttered by the centurion at the foot of Christ's cross for Christians to read two thousand years later. So, if God thought it important enough to highlight centurions in his Word, understanding more about who these men were and what they were like could prove to further enlighten our understanding of the passages in which these men play a part.

---

themselves and the military in which they fought, Julius Caesar's *The Civil War* and *The Gallic War* and invaluable resources.

3
THE ROMAN CENTURION AT THE CROSS

Matthew, Mark, and Luke all record that a centurion was overseeing the crucifixion of Jesus and spoke upon his death. Matthew and Mark wrote that the centurion said, "Truly this was the Son of God" or "Truly this man was the Son of God" while Luke tells us that the centurion said, "Certainly this man was innocent!"[1] Mark adds that the centurion was summoned by Pilate and asked if Jesus had already died, which the centurion confirmed.[2] This is all we know about this particular centurion. We have no details of his life, nor his other military service or beliefs. We do not know what this centurion did before he oversaw the crucifixion of Jesus nor what he did afterward. However, this man plays a major role in the narrative of Mark, and the fact that he was a centurion is central to the overall argument that Mark is making in his book.

The Centurion Who Crucified Christ

The simple fact is, we know very little about the Roman centurion who oversaw the crucifixion of Jesus. We know that he reported directly to Pontius Pilate as Mark records that Pilate was surprised at how quickly Jesus died and summoned the centurion to question him about Jesus' death.[3] Thus, the centurion was most likely connected directly to Pilate himself. The main military garrison in Judea was located in Caesarea Maritima, not in Jerusalem, and thus any Roman centurion reporting to Pilate would most likely have not been a member of the local garrison but could have been

---

[1] Matthew 27:54, Mark 15:39 and Luke 23:47.
[2] Mark 15:44.
[3] Mark 15:44.

Roman Centurions

a *centuriones frumentarii* or a soldier serving as a part of Pilate's small staff.[4] Another possibility is that this particular centurion did serve as a regular military centurion and that at least a cohort was permanently stationed in Jerusalem. This would fit with Acts 21:31–22:29, in which the Roman Tribune over a single cohort seems to lack a concrete understanding of Jewish religious customs when arresting Paul.[5] Thus, it could be that a small military garrison existed in Jerusalem several decades before Paul's arrest in the Temple, and Pilate had access to centurions from this garrison to carry out his executions.

The most likely scenario, however, is that this particular centurion was not Roman at all, but a local Palestinian who had come through the ranks of the army of Herod the Great.[6] As Jeffers notes, "The prefect of Judea commanded a small number of non-Roman auxiliary troops trained by Romans."[7] This, of course, fits with Shatzman's work that suggests Herod's army was organized and equipped after the manner of the Roman legions, and "a part of the Herodian army was eventually incorporated into the Roman *auxilia.*"[8] This means that the centurion who crucified Jesus was most likely Palestinian but would have been considered among the Samaritans, tax collectors, and other sinners according to the devout Jewish population at the time.

Another aspect to consider is that the Roman Army was religiously devout to the extreme. As D'Amato notes, "Religion was a fundamental aspect in the life of a centurion; these officers played a central role in the religious life of the army, which was

---

[4] J.R. McRay, "Caesarea Maritima," in *Dictionary of New Testament Background*, eds. Craig A. Evans & Stanley E. Porter (Downers Grove, IL: Intervarsity Press, 2000), 176-177; Hazel W. Perkin, "God-Fearer," in Baker Encyclopedia of the Bible (Grand Rapids, MI: Baker Book House, 1988), 888;

[5] Acts 21:31–22:29.

[6] Jeffers, *Greco-Roman World*, 128.

[7] Jeffers, *Greco-Roman World*, 128.

[8] Shatzman, *The Armies of the Hasmonaeans and Herod*, 198-205. See also pages 211 through 216.

intimately linked to the concept so hierarchy and loyalty."[9] The Roman military celebrated a plethora of religious festivals and feasts and had regularly scheduled religious ceremonies.[10] Each military camp had altars erected at its center, and the commanding officer's name of each unit was inscribed on these altars to represent the entire unit.[11] In each cohort, the name of the commanding officer would have been the chief centurion of the cohort. Further, according to Goldsworthy, "the military oath (*sacramentum*) had distinctly religious associations, so much so that the spirit of the oath (*genius sacramenti*) was occasionally venerated."[12] Finally, the worship of Rome's official gods and goddesses, as well as the imperial family, were a hallmark of proper Roman military service.[13] Given that Pontius Pilate was disposed to the cult of emperor worship, it is highly likely that the centurion who crucified Jesus was steeped in this pagan religious milieu and was almost certainly involved in various forms of idolatry, even if he was Palestinian in origin.[14]

In addition to the religious aspects of the Roman army, it is important to note that this particular centurion was not unaccustomed to extreme violence. The trademark symbol of a centurion was the *vitis*, or vine cane that was used to administer corporal punishment upon the soldiers under the centurion's command.[15] Roman soldiers were clubbed to death for falling asleep while on guard duty, and soldiers who fled from battle were "crucified or thrown to wild beasts."[16] Further, it is highly unlikely that this would have been the centurion's first crucifixion and he almost

---

[9] D'Amato, *Roman Centurions*, 18.
[10] Goldsworthy, *Complete Roman Army*, 108.
[11] Goldsworthy, *Complete Roman Army*, 108.
[12] Goldsworthy, *Complete Roman Army*, 109.
[13] Goldsworthy, *Complete Roman Army*, 109.
[14] Jeffers, *Greco-Roman World*, 130–131.
[15] Goldsworthy, *Complete Roman Army*, 101.
[16] Goldsworthy, *Complete Roman Army*, 101.

certainly participated in other forms of judicial punishment as well. If this centurion was a Roman, and a part of Pilate's staff, one of the purposes of his office could have been to execute those Pilate condemned to death. If the centurion was a *centuriones frumentarii*, then Law Enforcement and secret police action almost certainly involved torture and both judicial and extra-judicial punishment. However, as it is most likely that this centurion was a member of the *auxilia*, who reported to the prefect, it is likely that execution in general, and crucifixion in particular, were a regular part of the centurion's job.

There were fourteen governors of Judea between AD 6 and 66.[17] The prefect, or equestrian governor of Judea, reported directly to the legate, or senatorial governor of the province of Syria.[18] To further complicate matters, the territory of Judea was also ruled by local kings, the decendants of Herod the Great, who had pledged their allegiance to Rome.[19] It was during this period of time the Zealot party was active in Judea—as were the Essenes—and that the Roman authorities both confiscated the high priestly garments and appointed a succession of high priests in an effort to gain control over the Jewish population.[20] A soldier, whether a Roman from Italy or a Palestinian member of the *auxilia*, during this period of time would have most certainly been involved in various forms of military action as well as executing insurrectionists and others deemed criminals by the Roman or monarchical authorities. And any centurion reporting directly to the prefect of the province would most certainly have been involved in overseeing the execution of various individuals. The New Testament notes that the Jewish religious leaders were not allowed to execute anyone on their own, for they had to appeal to

---

[17] Jeffers, *Greco-Roman World*, 129.
[18] Jeffers, *Greco-Roman World*, 128.
[19] Jeffers, *Greco-Roman World*, 128.
[20] Jeffers, *Greco-Roman World*, 110–134.

Pilate to execute Jesus on their behalf, and also notes that the prefect was in the habit of annually releasing one prisoner condemned to death at the Passover celebration.[21] Both of these events suggest that executing prisoners was a regular part of army life in Judea and also for the centurion who executed Jesus.

So what do we know about the centurion who executed Jesus? We know that he was most likely a Palestinian centurion who was a member of the *auxilia*, and reported directly to Pilate. He was accustomed to violence, having had numerous opportunities to engage in military actions, and the execution of prisoners was almost certainly a routine part of his job. He was also heavily immersed in the pagan culture and religious worship of the Roman army. All of this would have combined to make this centurion a pariah among the average Jewish citizen living in Judea. Much like the tax collectors and Samaritans, this centurion would have been seen as being a part of the Roman system of oppression and would have been considered a traitor to his people and anathema in local society.

The Importance of the Centurion in Mark's Crucifixion Narrative

In his excellent commentary on the book of Mark, Mark Strauss notes that "Christology is on center stage throughout Mark's gospel and must be considered primary to his theological purpose."[22] Similarly, William Lane writes, "Throughout his entire Gospel, Mark bears witness to the word of revelation that Jesus is the Messiah, the Son of God," and James Edwards says, "The divine Sonship of Jesus is the theological keystone to the Gospel of Mark."[23]

---

[21] See Matthew 27, Mark 15, Luke 22-23, and John 18.

[22] Mark L. Strauss, *Mark*, Exegetical Commentary on the New Testament, vol. 2, ed. Clinton E. Arnold (Grand Rapids, MI: Zondervan, 2014), 41.

[23] William L. Lane, *The Gospel of Mark*, New International Commentary on the New Testament (Grand Rapids, MI: William B. Eerdmans Publishing Company, 1974), 1; James R. Edwards, *The Gospel According to Mark*, The Pillar New Testament

In other words, one of the primary points that Mark was trying to get across to his readers was that Jesus was, in fact, the Son of God. Again, Strauss argues that this is the primary theme of the first half of the book:

> The first half of this energetic story is characterized by three main themes: *authority*, *awe*, and *opposition*. Mark begins by identifying Jesus as "the Messiah, the Son of God" (1:1), and this messianic authority is on display at every turn. Jesus' message is the arrival of God's eschatological reign through his own words and deeds. He calls disciples, who drop everything to follow him; he captivates his hearers with remarkable teaching; he commands demons to come out of people, and they obey. He heals the sick with compassionate touch; he quiets a storm with a strong rebuke. The response to this is awe and wonder. The people are amazed at his authoritative teaching and his power over demons. They marvel when he heals the sick. The disciples stand in shock as he quiets the storm with a command. They wonder, "Who, then, is this, that the wind and the sea obey him!" (4:41).[24]

Strauss then goes on to argue that this theme climaxes with Peter's acknowledgment that Jesus is the Messiah, but the purpose of the second half of the gospel is to show that God's Messiah was not the Messiah that Peter, the Apostles, or the rest of the Jewish community were looking for.[25] So the overall purpose of the book of Mark is to show that Jesus is the Messiah and that the true Messiah came to suffer and die, not to conquer Rome in military victory.

One of the primary ways that Mark communicates the divinity of Christ is in the phrase "Son of God," which is repeated throughout the book. Mark calls Jesus the "Son of God" in the

---

Commentary (Grand Rapids, MI: Eerdmans, 2002), 15.
    [24] Strauss, *Mark*, 17.
    [25] Strauss, *Mark*, 18-20.

opening verse of his book.[26] At his baptism, God the Father announced that Jesus was his son when a voice from heaven declared, "You are my beloved Son, with you I am well pleased."[27] Then Jesus met a man in the synagogue possessed by unclean spirits and the spirits called Jesus "the Holy one of God."[28] Mark notes that when Jesus cast out demons, "he would not permit the demons to speak, because they knew him" or that they would fall down before him and cry out "you are the Son of God," but Jesus would order them "not to make him known."[29] While there is not enough room to cite every verse that traces this theme throughout Mark, the phrase "Son of God" is one that Mark used repeatedly.

Another theme that runs throughout the book of Mark is that the vast majority of people who interact with Jesus had no idea that Jesus was the Son of God. Even the disciples, who were the closest to Jesus, did not understand who Jesus really was. After Jesus calmed the storm, the disciples said, "Who then is this, that even the wind and the sea obey him?"[30] While Peter confessed that Jesus was "the Christ," afterward, he and the other disciples were rebuked by Jesus several times for their lack of understanding and blindness to who the Messiah really was.[31] Interestingly, Mark partially explains why Jesus' disciples did not understand who he was: "And he got into the boat with them, and the wind ceased. And they were utterly astounded, for they did not understand about the loaves, but *their hearts were hardened.*"[32]

What Mark is communicating here is that the hearts of the Jewish people, the religious leaders, and even the disciples, were hardened to the reality of Jesus' true identity. The evidence that

---

[26] Mark 1:1.
[27] Mark 1:11.
[28] Mark 1:24 and 3:11-12.
[29] Mark 1:34.
[30] Mark 4:41.
[31] Mark 8:27-33, 9:2-10, 9:30-32, and 10:32-45.
[32] Mark 6:51-52. Emphasis mine.

Roman Centurions

Jesus was the Son of God was overwhelming. The demons knew this reality and proclaimed it. God testified to Jesus' sonship on two separate occasions: once at his baptism and once at the transfiguration. The miracles that Jesus performed testified to the reality that Jesus is the Son of God, but the people either could not see it or were unable to see it. Either God had hardened their hearts, they had hardened their own hearts, or some combination of both, so that the people were blind to the reality of the divinity of Jesus. In fact, the only human person in all of Mark's gospel to proclaim out loud that Jesus was the Son of God is the centurion who oversaw his crucifixion.

The centurion most likely knew the stories about the Messiah. He also certainly knew the charges made against Jesus by the religious rulers because the inscription "King of the Jews" was nailed over Jesus' cross to declare the crime for which he was being punished.[33] This may not have even been the first insurrectionist the centurion had crucified. However, the manner in which Jesus died and the events surrounding his crucifixion were enough evidence for the centurion to say, "Truly this man was the Son of God!"[34] This centurion, who lived his life more in accordance with Roman cultural values than that of his birth, for whom torturing and killing other men was as routine as driving to work, and who spent countless hours worshiping at the altars of Roman deities, had enough evidence to shock him into the reality that Jesus was the Son of God.

The background of the centurion helps us to see the sharp contrast between him and the religious rulers. Mark is telling his readers that God declared Jesus to be divine, the demons declared Jesus to be divine, and the only person who grasped the divinity of Jesus was the centurion who crucified him.[35] The confession of

---

[33] Mark 15:26.
[34] Mark 15:39.
[35] Strauss, *Mark*, 705–706. This is not to suggest that the Centurion was somehow

the centurion highlights all the more the spiritual blindness of the disciples and religious rulers but also serves as a climactic moment in the overall narrative in the book of Mark.

As Strauss, Lane, and Edwards all noted, the main theme in the book of Mark is the divinity of Christ.[36] The book opens with Mark declaring that Jesus is the Son of God, and here ends with the centurion restating the same claim.[37] The centurion who crucified Jesus provides the final declaration in a book that highlights the divinity of Christ and his title as the Son of God. The fact that this declaration came from the centurion also serves to highlight both the universal nature of the evidence for Jesus' divinity and the universal nature of the salvation offered through Jesus' death and resurrection. Jesus' divinity was not something that was discovered and declared by a group of ultra-pious religious figures who then informed the rest of the world of their discovery. No one needed superior academic credentials to see that Jesus was the Son of God. If this centurion could figure it out, then certainly the evidence was overwhelming and obvious. In addition, this centurion was the most unlikely candidate to whom God would reveal anything miraculous. He was about as far from God as a Palestinian could be while he was alive. Yet, when everyone else had a hardened heart and was blind to the truth of Jesus Christ, God allowed this centurion to recognize the evidence for what it was. This, in part, serves to highlight that the centurion who crucified Jesus was, himself, an object lesson of Jesus' own words when he told the scribes, "I came not to call the righteous, but sinners."[38]

---

saved or that he grasped all of the implications of Jesus' divinity. It is only to state that the Centurion understood that Jesus was of divine origin.

[36] Strauss, *Mark*, 41; Lane, *The Gospel of Mark*, 1; Edwards, *The Gospel According to Mark*, 15.
[37] Mark 1:1 and 15:39.
[38] Mark 2:17.

4
THE ROMAN CENTURION CORNELIUS

The most prominent centurion mentioned in the New Testament is a man named Cornelius, who the book of Acts says, was "a centurion of what was known as the Italian Cohort, a devout man who feared God with all his household, gave alms generously to the people, and prayed continually to God."[1] Acts also describes Cornelius as "a centurion, an upright and God-fearing man, who is well spoken of by the whole Jewish nation."[2] Why, then, does the text mention that Cornelius is a centurion? The book of Acts could very well have mentioned that Cornelius was "a devout man who feared God with all his household, gave alms generously to the people, and prayed continually to God" as well as being "an upright and God-fearing man, who is well spoken of by the whole Jewish nation."[3] In other words, Luke (the author of the book of Acts) could very well have left out the fact that Cornelius was a centurion without changing anything about how we read the text. So, why does Luke mention that Cornelius was a centurion, and what is this information supposed to convey to the reader?

Who Was Cornelius?
The very first thing that is mentioned about Cornelius in the book of Acts is that he was "a centurion of what was known as the Italian Cohort."[4] First, Roman legionary soldiers were recruited heavily from Italy until the mid-1st century, and thus Cornelius

---
[1] Acts 10:1–2.
[2] Acts 10:22.
[3] Acts 10:1–2 and 10:22.
[4] Acts 10:1.

was probably from Italy himself.[5] No historical evidence exists about an Italian Cohort in any of the literature that has survived to date. However, it is important to note that Luke records that Cornelius' Cohort was actually given the title of "Italian Cohort" by the people at the time.[6] This seems to suggest that the other Cohorts in the Legion were not primarily composed of recruits from Italy as opposed to the Cohort that Cornelius belonged to. Further, the retired and active military soldiers in Judea during this period would largely have been Jewish and have served under the Herodian military force.[7] In addition, although some centurions would have married local women, far more Herodian centurions would have lived in the area than active or retired Roman centurions. Thus, to start with, Luke is trying to communicate that Cornelius is not a Jewish centurion. Cornelius was not a part of God's covenant people as understood by the Jewish community and the Old Testament, a point that proves critical to understanding the larger narrative and especially Peter's dream and response.

The second detail of Cornelius that can be inferred from the text is that Cornelius was most likely one of the top five centurions of the entire legion and possibly the *primus pilus*, or chief centurion in the legion. As mentioned earlier, Roman infantry was organized into different combat units called legions, which were comprised of 10 cohorts, which were made up of six *centuriae*, and each *centuria* had a strength of 80 men and was commanded by a centurion.[8] In the case of Cornelius, he was a part of a unit made up of approximately 800 men who had largely been recruited from Italy. In garrison, each centurion had a private room at the end of their *centuria's* barracks building in the military camp, and the

---

[5] D'Amato, *Roman Centurions*, 6; Cowan, *Roman Legionary*, 11.
[6] Acts 10:1.
[7] Shatzman, *The Armies of the Hasmonaeans and Herod*, 186–205.
[8] Goldsworthy, *Roman Army at War*, 13.

senior centurion of the cohort lived among them as well.[9] However, Cornelius lived with "his household" rather than in a barracks.[10] The centurions of the first cohort, which was made up of the best soldiers and considered the highest-ranked cohort in a legion, were allowed to live in small houses rather than live in the barracks with their soldiers.[11] Thus, it stands to reason that because Cornelius was living with his household, the Italian Cohort was the first cohort in their legion. This would have made Cornelius among the top five centurions in the legion. Now, the book of Acts notes that Cornelius was "a centurion of what was known as the Italian Cohort."[12] While this is slightly ambiguous language in that it suggests Cornelius could have been the senior centurion of the group, it is more likely that he was one of the seven other centurions that belonged to the Italian Cohort. If Cornelius has been the *primus pilus* or senior centurion of the entire legion, it would be more likely that Luke would have titled him as such rather than referring to him as "*a centurion* of what was known as the Italian Cohort."[13] However, it is probable that Cornelius was among the top centurions in his legion, if not the *primus pilus* and thus was fairly senior in rank.

This, of course, means that Cornelius would have spent most of his adult life participating in the same pagan religious ceremonies discussed in the previous chapter. In fact, given that Cornelius was a rather senior centurion, he most likely spent a great deal of his career in the military participating and even leading religious ceremonies to worship the military standard, the Emperor, the royal family, and various other Roman deities.[14] Like the cen-

---

[9] Goldsworthy, *Complete Roman Army*, 82–86.
[10] Acts 10:2.
[11] Goldsworthy, *Complete Roman Army*, 86.
[12] Acts 10:1.
[13] Acts 10:1. Emphasis mine.
[14] Goldsworthy, *Complete Roman Army*, 108–109.

turion who crucified Jesus, Cornelius also would have been accustomed to seeing and acting in violence.[15] Using corporal punishment on the soldiers under his command, and dealing violence against anyone declared an enemy force by his superior officers, would have been routine for Cornelius. Further, for Cornelius to have risen so far through the ranks means that he had to have been well thought of by his senior military officers and been exceptionally proficient at dealing with the violence his profession demanded. What is striking, however, is that Cornelius was described by Luke as a man who "feared God."[16] This is the first indication that Cornelius is not going to fit the typical profile of a Roman centurion serving in Judea.

Scott McKnight tells us that "Godfearer" is a term used by Jews in the 1st century to refer to Gentiles "who honor God in various ways (including almsgiving and synagogue participation) who are distinguished from run-of-the-mill Gentiles, and the term seems to be nearly synonymous with 'proselyte' or a category of proselytes."[17] McKnight goes on, however, note that "for Luke, the Godfearer is a quasi-official sympathizer with Judaism."[18] This much has already been made clear by Luke's text itself as Luke stated that Cornelius "gave alms generously to the people, and prayed continually to God."[19] However, being a Godfearer still meant being separate from the Jewish nation, and specifically prohibited from worship at the temple.[20]

There are a number of possible explanations for Cornelius being a man who "feared God.[21] First, as it was entirely appropriate

---

[15] Goldsworthy, *Complete Roman Army*, 101.
[16] Acts 10:2.
[17] Scott McKnight, "Proselytism and Godfearers," in *Dictionary of New Testament Background*, ed. Craig A. Evans and Stanley E. Porter (Downers Grove, IL: Intervarsity Press, 2000), 846.
[18] McKnight, "Proselytism and Godfearers," 846.
[19] Acts 10:1.
[20] McKnight, "Proselytism and Godfearers," 839–840.
[21] Acts 10:2.

for centurions to marry local women, Cornelius could very well have married a local Jewish woman and thus come under the influence of the religious beliefs of her and her family.[22] As Cornelius lived in the military garrison in Caesarea Maritima, it is also possible that he simply came under the influence of local religious teaching and that God opened his eyes to the true faith. Caesarea Maritima had a large Jewish population, and Cornelius probably participated in the Jewish synagogue in the city as much as was allowed a Gentile convert.[23] No matter how Cornelius came to understand the truth of the Jewish faith at the time, the New Testament describes Cornelius as a man who "feared God" and who was "well-spoken of by the whole Jewish nation."[24]

The Importance of Cornelius the Centurion

Cornelius is an integral part of the larger story in Acts 10 in which Peter is given a vision by God and instructed that the gospel was open to Gentiles as well as Jews. At the beginning of chapter 10, the reader is introduced to Cornelius and told that he received a visit from an angel who instructed Cornelius to send for "Simon who is called Peter" from the house of "Simon, a tanner, whose house is by the sea" in Joppa.[25] Joppa was approximately 60km south of Caesarea Maritima, where Cornelius lived. Luke goes on to tell us, "the next day, as they [the men sent by Cornelius to find Peter] were on their journey and approaching the city," Peter had a vision from God while he was in prayer.[26] In Peter's vision, God showed him all kinds of unclean animals and commanded Peter to eat. When Peter refused, God rebuked him and told Peter, "what

---

[22] Goldsworthy, *Complete Roman Army*, 103-104.
[23] J.R. McRay, "Caesarea Maritima," in *Dictionary of New Testament Background*, 888.
[24] Acts 10:2 and 22.
[25] Acts 10:1-8.
[26] Acts 10:9.

God has made clean, do not call common."²⁷ After Peter's vision, Cornelius' men arrived and Peter went with them back to Caesarea to see Cornelius. Interestingly, even upon entering Cornelius' house, Peter felt compelled to tell Cornelius, "You yourselves know how unlawful it is for a Jew to associate with or to visit anyone of another nation. But God has shown me that I should not call any person common or unclean."²⁸ However, when Cornelius told Peter about his visit from the angel, Peter understood that he was sent to share the gospel with Cornelius and then baptized him and his household after they heard the gospel and believed.²⁹ Cornelius and his household were the first group of Gentiles to be brought into the Christian faith. Through this entire event, God was instructing Peter and the early church that the gospel was open to Gentiles, and, as Peter said, "in every nation anyone who fears him and does what is right is acceptable to him."³⁰

One thing that is important to note about Cornelius is his status as a Godfearer and his status as a centurion. It is interesting to note Peter's reaction upon entering Cornelius' house. Peter had been told that Cornelius was a Godfearer and that he was well-thought-of by the Jews. This is evident in that when Peter tells Cornelius about how unlawful it is to be inside of his home, Peter already expects Cornelius to know this information. One might not expect a pagan from Corinth to know about Jewish religious norms, but a Godfearer would be expected to know what was acceptable and unacceptable for a pious Jew. Yet, Peter still regards Cornelius as being unclean and was only persuaded to step into Cornelius' house because of a vision from God. However, from a contemporary perspective, it does not seem at all shocking that a Godfearer would be one of the first Gentiles to be brought into the

---

[27] Acts 10:9–16.
[28] Acts 10:28.
[29] Acts 10:30–48.
[30] Acts 10:34.

Cornelius

Christian fold. In fact, it was probably less shocking for Peter to be sent to give the gospel to a Godfearer than had God sent Peter to preach the gospel to the Gentiles in Corinth. However, Peter is still somewhat reluctant to preach to Cornelius, and his status as a centurion may have something to do with Peter's initial reaction.

Caesarea Maritima was the central location for Roman Hellenization in Judea. Caesarea Maritima was constructed over an old city by Herod the Great and was "entirely rebuilt with white stone, and adorned with the most magnificent palaces, displaying here, as nowhere else, the innate grandeur of his character."[31] By the time of Peter's visit, Herod's palace in the city had become the *praetorium*, or headquarters for the Roman governor of Syria, and this is most likely the building where Paul met with Felix after being arrested.[32] The city itself was modeled after other major Roman cities, and Roman values would have permeated the city's architecture and culture.[33] The city was also a center for the larger regional conflict between the Syrians and the Jews, and as the city was such a mixture of cultural and religious customs, it is easy to see how Peter would be on guard when interacting with even supposed Godfearers in a place like this.[34] Add to this the fact that Cornelius was a centurion and a very high-ranking one at that. Cornelius could only have risen through the ranks by participating in the Hellenistic culture and practices of the military, and certainly was exceptional in his embrace of Judaism.

All of this background information, when combined, helps the contemporary reader to see exactly what Luke was trying to get across to his audience when he wrote the book of Acts. The larger

---

[31] Josephus, *Jewish Antiquities*, 1.21.5, as cited by J.R. McRay, "Caesarea Maritima," *Dictionary of New Testament Background*, ed., Craig S. Evans and Stanley E. Porter (Downers Grove, IL: Intervarsity Press, 2000), 176.

[32] McRay, "Caesarea Maritima," 176.

[33] McRay, "Caesarea Maritima," 176.

[34] McRay, "Caesarea Maritima," 176.

narrative focuses on God's gift of opening the gospel to the Gentiles. It makes sense, along these lines, that a Godfearer would be the first to hear the gospel as it would be much easier for the early Jewish-background Christians to accept a Godfearer into the fold than someone from a completely pagan background. However, it is important to note that by choosing Cornelius, God was pushing Peter and the early church to understand that the gospel was open to everyone. God started with a Godfearer, but a Godfearer from about as offensive a background that a good Palestinian Jew could imagine at the time. Thus, God chose the centurion Cornelius to hear and believe the gospel in order to stretch Peter's faith, as well as the faith of the other early Jewish background Chritians. However, Cornelius' integration into the church did not prematurely force the early church leadership to deal with issues common among pagan background beleivers like those Paul would later address in his letter to the Corinthians.[35] Further along in the book of Acts, we see that the church eventually had to come to grips with integrating believers from completely pagan backgrounds with the Jewish-background Christians, but God allowed this to be a slow process and, in Cornelius, gave the early church time and grace in coming to this realization.

Finally, there is one last observation about Cornelius that warrants further exploration but might suggest another reason that the centurion Cornelius was included in Luke's book. It is known that Luke was a physician and wrote both Luke and Acts to a man named Theophilus.[36] Physicians in the Roman world were usually slaves who were educated as physicians to provide medical service to their masters.[37] Another interesting fact about the Roman world is that when a person had a close relationship with someone,

---

[35] Paul addressed a number of issues in his letter to the Cornithians such as immoral sexual practices, eating food offered to idols, and continuing in pagan religious practices that were common issues pagan background believers had to grapple with. Cornelius did not come to the faith thinking these types of practices were acceptable and thus Peter and the early church were not forced to address how to rightly think about such things.

[36] Luke 1:3 and Acts 1:1 ESV.

[37] Michael Haykin, "The Ancient Church in its Graeco-Roman Context," Lecture Series, The Southern Baptist Theological Seminary (Louisville, KY, Fall 2018).

they often referred to them by a lengthened name rather than a more formal short name.[38] In each of Paul's three letters (Romans, 1 Corinthians, and 2 Timothy), Paul greets a woman named Prisca.[39] Luke, on the other hand, refers to the same woman by the name of Priscilla throughout the book of Acts.[40] This indicates that Luke probably had a closer relationship with Priscilla than Paul did. This also makes it entirely plausible that Luke, Priscilla, and Theophilus all had some sort of relationship with one another.[41] Perhaps Theophilus was Priscilla's father or another relative. Perhaps Luke was a slave of Priscilla's family but was then sent with Paul on his missionary journeys. While this all warrants more investigation, an interesting fact about Luke's narrative in his books is his constant mention of high-ranking and prominent individuals.[42] Luke places all of these events on a timeline that includes when high ranking individuals were in office, where they were located, and who the early Christians interacted with. In this case, Luke could very well have included Cornelius the centurion, and the information about him, in a similar manner. It is not implausible to suggest that Theophilus could have followed up with Cornelius by writing a letter at a later date. Another possibility, assuming Theophilus was wealthy and well-connected enough to send a slave on a multi-year fact-finding mission to write about the

---

[38] Haykin, Lecture Notes. This is quite the opposite from what we do today. Today, in a more formal setting a person may be called Jonathan but could be called John or Johnny by his friends. In the Roman world, the opposite was true. A more formal name would be John while the less formal name would be Jonathan.

[39] Haykin, "The Ancient Church," Lecture Series; Romans 16:3, 1 Corinthians 16:19, and 2 Timothy 4:19.

[40] Haykin, "The Ancient Church," Lecture Series; Acts 18:2, 18:18 and 18:26 ESV.

[41] It is, of course, also possible that Luke's use of the less formal Priscilla had to do more with the letter's intended audience rather than the author. If this is the case, then is makes sense that Paul, even if he commonly called Priscilla by her less formal name, would have used her more formal name given that he was writing to entire churches in his letters. This would then suggest, as Luke is writing to Theophilus and not an entire church body, that Theophilus and Priscilla probably knew each other well.

[42] See Luke 1:5, Luke 2:1, and Acts 24:1-23 as examples.

history of the early church, that Theophilus may have known some of Cornelius' commanding officers or other patrons. While there may not be enough information available to answer some of these questions, it is one potential avenue for future investigation.

5
THE ROMAN CENTURION, HIS SERVANT, AND ACTS

Both Matthew 8 and Luke 7 recount a story of the centurion who asked Jesus to heal his servant. In both accounts, the centurion has a servant who is extremely ill and asks Jesus to intervene on his servant's behalf.[1] In both books, Jesus begins to go visit the ill servant but is stopped by the centurion who tells Jesus that he is not worthy to have Jesus come to his home and that he knows, as a man under authority, that all Jesus needs to do is speak a word and the servant will be healed.[2] Both times, Jesus praises the centurion, commends him for his faith, and heals his servant from afar.[3]

We know less about this centurion than either of the previous two. Both Matthew and Luke note that Jesus was in Capernaum when these events took place, so the centurion must have lived nearby.[4] Archaeologists have discovered the remains of what they believe to be the synagogue that was built by the centurion and in which Jesus preached.[5] But there is no large military garrison in Capernaum, nor anywhere close by. The next likely location for a centurion to be located was in the city of Tiberius, which was the governmental headquarters for the region of Galilee.[6] It is probable that this centurion was stationed in Capernaum, along with a small military contingent, in order to collect taxes and generally

---

[1] Matthew 8:5-7 and Luke 7:3-5.
[2] Matthew 8:8-9 and Luke 7:6-8.
[3] Matthew 8:10-13 and Luke 7:9-10.
[4] Matthew 8 and Luke 7.
[5] Anson F. Rainey and R. Steven Notley, *The Sacred Bridge: Carta's Atlas of the Biblical World*, 2nd emended and enhanced ed. (Jerusalem: CARTA, 2014), 355-356.
[6] Rainey & Notley, *The Sacred Bridge*, 354-355.

keep order. Robert Gundry suggests that the term "centurion" was being used loosely by both Matthew and Luke because the military garrison in Tiberius would have been Herodian in origin, but, as has already been shown, the Herodian army was modeled after the Roman army and thus would have had officers with the title of centurion.[7] Further, centurions were put in command of *frumentarii* soldiers who would have been stationed away from their main legion and conducted law enforcement activities.[8] Thus, this centurion was most likely Palestinian in origin and served in the Herodian Army or as a member of the Roman *auxilia*.

The Importance of This Centurion in Matthew

One of the overall purposes that Matthew had for writing his gospel was as an apologetic and evangelistic message to a Jewish audience.[9] This can be seen in how Matthew organized his gospel and how he communicated the story of Jesus to his readers, which the story of Jesus healing the centurion's servant is a part.[10] Osborne notes that "the emphasis is not so much on the miracle as on the centurion's 'great faith' in humbly placing himself under Jesus' authority. He thereby becomes an example of the place of faithful Gentiles in the kingdom and a contrast to unfaithful Israel that will be outside God's mercy."[11] Matthew is also communicating that because God's people have rejected Jesus, "he will now fulfill [the Abrahamic covenant] through the new Israel, the church."[12]

---

[7] Robert Gundry, *Matthew: A Commentary on His Literary and Theological Art* (Grand Rapids, MI: Eerdmans, 1982), 141; Shatzman, *The Armies of the Hasmonaeans and Herod*, 198–205.

[8] D'Amato, *Roman Centurions*, 7.

[9] Grant R. Osborne, *Matthew*, Zondervan Exegetical Commentary on the New Testament, ed. Clinton E. Arnold (Grand Rapids, MI: Zondervan, 2010), 31.

[10] Osborne, *Matthew*, 31-33.

[11] Osborne, *Matthew*, 287.

[12] Osborne, *Matthew*, 295.

The Centurion, his Servant, and Acts

The centurion, then, in Matthew is a picture of God's coming grace to the Gentile community, and the centurion's background is critical to communicating this to the Jewish audience to whom Matthew was writing. No one reading Matthew's gospel would have mistaken the centurion for a Jew. As previously discussed, the religious and cultural milieu that centurions generally lived in, the extreme violence that these men were exposed to, and their status in Judea as being a part of the system oppressing the Jews all served to identify these men as outsiders to Matthew's Jewish audience.[13] The role the centurion plays in the narrative then is critical in helping the primarily Jewish audience to understand that the gospel is open to all who desire to submit themselves to Jesus.

The Importance of This Centurion in Luke

The same story has a slightly different purpose in the Gospel of Luke, and perhaps the best explanation of the overall purpose of the gospel is provided by Darrell Bock in the introduction to his two-volume commentary. Bock writes:

> It is unlikely that Theophilus is just interested in becoming a Christian or is a Roman official who needs to have Christianity explained in order to accept it as a legitimate religion. Nor are Paul and his message of simple evangelism the object of defense. Too little of the Gospel deals with such legal, political concerns and too much exhortation deals with issues beyond simple evangelism. Paul is important to the last part of Acts only because of the mission and perspective he represents. Luke 1:3–4 suggests that Theophilus received some instruction. The detail in Luke-Acts about faithfulness, Jew-Gentile relations, and clinging to the hope of Jesus' return suggests a Gentile who is experiencing doubt about his association with the new community. The

---

[13] Goldsworthy, *Complete Roman Army*, 108–109.

problems over table fellowship, Gentile inclusion, and examples of how rejection was faced in the early church also suggest this setting. Likewise, the amount of ethical exhortation in the Gospel suggests this approach. Theophilus appears to be a man of rank (Luke 1:3) who has associated himself with the church, but doubts whether in fact he really belongs in this racially mixed and heavily persecuted community. In the Gospel, Luke takes Theophilus through Jesus' career in order to review how God worked to legitimize Jesus and how Jesus proclaimed hope. Luke also wishes to defend God's faithfulness to Israel and his promises, despite the rejection of the promise by many in the nation. (In this sense, Luke is not unlike Rom. 9–11.) The offer of the gospel openly includes Theophilus and calls him to remain faithful, committed, and expectant, even in the midst of intense Jewish rejection and with the hope that both Jews and Gentiles will turn to Jesus. What is very possible is that Theophilus had been a God-fearer before coming to Christ, since this can explain the interest in God-fearers in Acts (10:2, 22, 35; 13:16, 26, 43, 50; 17:4, 17; 18:7), as well as the extensive use of the OT in the two volumes.[14]

The purpose of the gospel, then, was to help boost Theophilus' confidence in what he had been taught concerning Christianity and encourage him to hold onto the faith. This, in turn, means the story of Jesus healing the centurion's servant fits within this overall purpose.

Bock notes that "the healing of the centurion's slave in Luke 7:1–10 foreshadow[s] the expansion of Jesus' ministry to the nations," but Matthew Easter argues that the three centurions in Luke's gospel "form a 'narrative chain' linking people of exem-

---

[14] Darrel L. Bock, *Luke: 1:1–9:50*, Baker Exegetical Commentary on the New Testament, ed. Moisés Silva (Grand Rapids, MI: Baker Publishing Group, 1994), 14–15.

plary faith" and that Luke's concern in writing about this centurion was "to highlight [this] faith."[15] Thus, Luke is not trying to point out that the Abrahamic Covenant was now open to Gentiles as Matthew did, but is trying to point out the centurion's unique and exemplary faith in Christ.[16] This fits in the overall intent of the book, according to Bock, and is also in line with Jesus' response to the centurion in the narrative.

Other Centurions in the Book of Acts

The book of Acts also records several other centurions who interacted with the Apostle Paul on different occasions. Paul was rescued by a centurion in the temple while he was being beaten by the Jews.[17] Most likely, the same centurion then intervened with the Tribune to prevent Paul from being whipped because he was a Roman citizen.[18] A centurion again intervenes on Paul's behalf to take an informant to a tribune and report on a plot against Paul's life.[19] Two centurions are charged with protecting Paul while he was being transported to Caesarea Maritima to see Felix the Governor.[20] A centurion is put in charge of Paul while he is in prison, but is charged to show Paul lenient treatment.[21] Finally, in Acts 27, a centurion named Julius, of the Augustan Cohort, was charged with escorting Paul to Rome.[22] According to the narrative, Julius initially does not take Paul's advice but through a

---

[15] Bock, *Luke*, 644; Matthew C. Easter, "'Certainly This Man Was Righteous': Highlighting a Messianic Reading of the Centurion's Confession in Luke 23:47," *Tyndale Bulletin* 63, no. 1 (2012): 41.

[16] While Easter argued that this was a saving faith, I do not think we can quite get there from the text. However, I do think that Luke was trying to communicate that the Centurion placed an extraordinary amount of faith in Jesus, as Jesus noted himself.

[17] Acts 21:32.
[18] Acts 22:25–26.
[19] Acts 23:17–22.
[20] Acts 23:23.
[21] Acts 24:23.
[22] Acts 27.

storm and a shipwreck learns to trust what Paul has to say.[23]

The Importance of These Centurions

The first thing to note about these centurions is that most are completely unimportant in themselves. They simply serve a larger purpose in the overall story in protecting Paul and providing for the advancement of the gospel. This illustrates that not all centurions in the New Testament play an integral part in the story and that the background of each one is not necessarily important. Luke was, after all, writing as a historian and sometimes simply recorded the facts. Centurions were a part of everyday life in the 1st century, and thus the fact that some of these men were centurions is completely inconsequential to the story or the overall narrative.

However, it is interesting to note that every centurion in the New Testament is portrayed favorably. The only negative mention of any centurion in the entire New Testament is when Luke records that Julius did not initially listen to Paul.[24] However, by the end of the journey, Julius had learned to trust Paul and even to care for him. This is strikingly odd given that soldiers in general, and centurions in particular, were not necessarily known as being kind-hearted individuals who treated the non-Roman population favorably. So, why then, do we see nothing but favorable accounts of centurions throughout the New Testament?

First, the centurion who crucified Christ was a historical person and was included in Mark, Matthew, and Luke because his presence and statement served the large purposes of their individual narratives. Mark wanted to highlight the centurion's confession that Jesus was the "Son of God," Matthew wanted to highlight that the gospel was now available to the Gentiles, and Luke wanted to highlight the faith of the centurion himself. The only

---

[23] Acts 27..
[24] Acts 27:11.

The Centurion, his servant, and Acts

other centurion mentioned outside of Luke's writings is Matthew's account of the centurion who asked Jesus to heal his servant. As discussed earlier in the chapter, Matthew included this centurion in his narrative because it served to instruct his primarily Jewish audience that the gospel was now open to the Gentile community. Only Luke writes about the additional five to six centurions that we read about in the New Testament.

We know from Luke's books that he was writing to a man named Theophilus.[25] We know that Theophilus was most likely wealthy, that he could have been connected to Priscila, and that he was connected with the early church.[26] It is also highly probable that for Luke—a physician and historian—to be traveling with Paul and writing a first-hand history of Jesus and the early church, he had to have been financed by a wealthy and well-connected patron. As Bock mentioned, we also know that Luke's purpose in writing to Theophilus was to shore up his confidence in what he had been taught concerning Christianity and encourage him to hold onto the faith.[27] One possible explanation then, for the inclusion of so many centurions in his books, is that Theophilus was himself either a centurion or a former centurion.

As Goldsworthy notes, "centurions were extremely important individuals who might be given positions of considerable responsibility. Some were appointed to administer regions of a province where they were the most senior representative of Roman rule."[28] Centurions were also very wealthy compared to the general population and the average Roman soldier. Pliny the Younger secured a commission as a centurion for one of his clients and provided the man with 40,000 sesterces to get him started in his profession.[29]

---

[25] Luke 1:3 and Acts 1:1.
[26] Luke 1:1–3 and Acts 1:1; Bock, *Luke*, 14–15.
[27] Bock, *Luke*, 14–15.
[28] Goldsworthy, *Complete Roman Army*, 72.
[29] Goldsworthy, *Complete Roman Army*, 72.

ROMAN CENTURIONS

This was more money than the average Roman soldier would make in an entire 25-year career.[30] Centurions could also be wealthy enough to have slaves, families, and even their own houses.[31] It is certainly possible then that Luke includes so many accounts of centurions having great faith, and centurions performing good deeds for the early church because Luke was trying to encourage the centurion Theophilus to continue in his Christian faith and "press on toward the goal for the prize of the upward call of God in Christ Jesus."[32] If true, this would go a long way to explain the importance of the accounts of the various centurions in the New Testament and explain their universally favorable representation among the New Testament authors.

---

[30] Goldsworthy, *Complete Roman Army*, 72.

[31] Matthew 8, Luke 7 and Acts 10. The Roman Centurion who asked Jesus to heal his servant was wealthy enough to have a servant, or more likely a slave; and Cornelius was wealthy enough to have his own household. In addition, both men were wealthy enough to finance the building of synagogues for their local Jewish communities.

[32] Philippians 3:14.

Conclusion

Roman centurions appear at some very critical moments in the New Testament. Centurions are held up as great examples of faith, as in the centurion who asked Jesus to heal his servant. Mark uses a centurion as an example to highlight the clarity of the evidence for the divinity of Christ. A centurion was also used by Matthew as an example of the Gentile community to which the early church was commissioned to take the gospel. At every turn of Paul's final journey, centurions intervene to protect him and ensure that Paul will be able to preach the gospel in Rome. Yet, centurions are often overlooked by scholars who assume that centurions are just another character in a larger story.

    The fact that certain individuals are titled as centurions in the New Testament provides important context and background information to the larger narrative of the biblical books in which they are found. This is not to suggest that historical scholarship on centurions is critical to properly interpreting the Bible. Rather, historical scholarship on centurions provides a certain level of background information to help the preacher or New Testament scholar to properly place the scripture in its historical context. The overall message of God's plan of salvation and eternal life offered through Jesus Christ is not changed or altered in any way by a greater understanding of Roman centurions. However, a greater understanding of Roman centurions does provide the preacher or New Testament scholar with background information to help discern the authorial intent of some biblical books and the overall purpose of some biblical passages. These men are propped up as illustrations and models of faith by the biblical authors and their being centurions is key to understanding why these particular men are being used as examples. In short, if it was important enough to the biblical authors, inspired by the Holy Spirit, to mention that an individual was a Roman centurion, then it is equally important for contemporary scholars to understand who Roman centurions are in order to properly understand why the biblical authors thought necessary to point out the person's title in the first place.

While this book begins to move in the right direction, scholars should continue to look to advances made in Roman military scholarship and compare these accounts with the New Testament record. Where Roman military scholarship seems to diverge from the New Testament, it is right to hold up the authority of the Bible over an ever-changing and advancing historiography. However, where Roman historical studies provide insight into the biography of Roman centurions, or other New Testament figures, these should be explored and incorporated into New Testament studies to help futher our understanding of the 1st-century world in which the biblical authors lived and wrote.

About the Author

Steven Mercer first became interested in Roman Centurions while serving as a Green Beret with the U.S. Army's 5th Special Forces Group; also known as "The Legion." 5th Group's motto is "Strength and Honor" and soldiers often have the letters "SPQR" on t-shirts or embroidered on patches as a way to connect with the values and ethos of the Roman Legions. After more than 12 years of military service, Steven left the Army to attend The Southern Baptist Theological Seminary. When the opportunity arose to take a course on "The New Testament in it's Graeco-Roman Context" with Dr. Michael A. G. Haykin, the stage for this book was set.

After his seminary studies, Steven moved to Uganda to serve on the mission field with Samaritan's Purse International Relief. Led by Franklin Graham, Samaritan's Purse is a non-profit Christian aid ministry that seeks to help meet the needs of people who are victims of war, poverty, natural disasters, disease, and famine with the purpose of sharing God's love through His Son, Jesus Christ. Steven currently serves as the Director of International Security for Samaritan's Purse and oversees the safety and security of all ministry activity outside of the United States.

Steven holds a Bachelor of Arts degree in History from the University of Maryland University College and both the Master of Divinity in Christian Ministry and Master of Theology in Christian Missions degrees from Southern Seminary. He currently lives in Boone, North Carolina with his wife Caroline and their six children, without whom none of the above would have been possible or worthwhile. Steven enjoys bow hunting, reading good books, traveling to unique places, spending time with his family, and sharing the gospel with anyone who will listen.

Index

A

Administration, 23, 29, 30, 31, 35, 36, 37, 38
Artillery, 8, 10, 25

C

Caesar Augustus, 29
Castus, 33
Cavalry, 8, 10, 13
Chiliarch, 13
Citizenship, 24
Clothing, 7, 15, 24
Constantine, 11
Cornelius, 3, 5, 6, 9, 12, 13, 18, 38, 51, 52, 53, 54, 55, 56, 57, 58, 68, 79
Crucifixion, 5, 9, 41, 43, 44, 45, 48

D

Decurion, 13
Desertion, 27

E

Equestrian Order, 31
Essenes, 44
Execution, 15, 42, 44, 45

G

Gentiles, 54, 55, 56, 58, 62, 64, 65, 66

H

Hellenization, 37, 57
Herod Antipas, 13
Herod the Great, 20, 42, 44, 57
Herodian Army, 7, 20, 62
Heroism, 27, 28

I

Infantry, 8, 10, 23, 26, 52
Insurrection, 48
Italian Cohort, 5, 51, 53

J

Jewish Revolt, 19
Julianus, Julius, 34, 35
Julius Caesar, 8, 10, 28, 31, 38, 81
Justice, 32, 33

L

Literacy, 2, 13, 15, 25, 28, 32
Liustinus, Spurius, 10
Living conditions, 19
Loyalty, 43

M

Marcellinus, Aurelius Julius, 33
Marcianus, Aurelius, 32, 33
Marriage, 17, 18, 37, 38, 52, 55
Medical care, 24
Mistreatment, 36

O

Ortiago, 36

P

Pacifism, 11
Passover, 45
Paternus, Ammonius, 32
Petekas, Syrus, 32
Petronius, Marcus, 28, 29
Pilate, 37, 41, 43, 44, 45
Pliny the Younger, 67
Police, 14, 23, 31, 32, 33, 34, 44
Polybius, 8, 12, 13
Praetorian Guard, 5, 11, 16, 17, 81
Priscilla, 59
Promotion, 15, 16, 25, 29, 31, 32, 36, 37
Punishment, 18, 33, 43, 44, 54

R

Rape, 7
Retirement, 18, 24
Roman Empire, 1, 23, 31, 33, 80

S

Salary, 13, 18, 35, 68
Sarapion, Aurelius, 32
Scaeva, 27
Sickness, 24, 46
Slavery, 58, 59, 60, 64, 68
Stature, 15, 25
Status, 15, 16, 17, 18, 23, 24, 28, 56, 57, 63

T

Taxes, 32, 61
Theophilus, 58, 59, 63, 64, 67, 68
Tisais, Aurelia, 33
Titanianus, Valerius, 33
Training, 13, 14, 19, 24, 25, 26

W

Warfare, 10, 11, 18, 19, 25, 26
Women, 17, 18, 32, 37, 38, 52, 55, 59

Scripture Index

New Testament

Matthew
8 ....59, 66
8:5–7 59
8:5–13 .... 6, 77, 78
8:8–9 59
8:10–13 59
10:18 35
27 43
27:2 35
27:11 35
27:14 35
27:15 35
27:21 35
27:27 35
27:54 .... 5, 39
28:14 35

Mark
1:1 .... 45, 47
1:11 45
1:24 45
1:34 45
2:17 47
3:11-12 45
4:41 45
6:51–52 45
8:27–33 45
9:2–10 45
9:30–32 45
10:32–45 45
13:9 35
15   43

15:26 46
15:39 .... 5, 39, 46, 47
15:44 39
15:44–45 5

Luke
1:1–3 65
1:3 .... 56, 61, 62, 65
1:5 57
2:1 57
3:1 35
7 .... 12, 59, 66
7:1 62
7:3–5 59
7:6–8 59
7:9–10 59
20:20 35
23:47 .... 5, 39, 63, 75

John
18 43

Acts
1:1 .... 56, 65
10 .... 12, 66
10:1 .... 49, 50, 51, 52
10:2 .... 51, 52, 53, 62
10:9 53
10:22 .... 49, 53
10:28 54
10:34 54
10:1-2 49
10:1–22 5

10:1–8	53
10:30–48	54
10:34–43	7, 76
10:9–16	54
13:16	62
17:4	62
18:2	57
18:7	62
18:18	57
18:26	57
21:32	5, 63
21:31–22	40
22:24–29	34
22:25–26	5, 63
23:17–22	63
23:23	63
23:24	35
23:26	35
23:33	35
24:1–23	57
24:23	63
26:30	35
27:1–43	34
27:11	64

Romans

9–11	62
16:3	57

1 Corinthians

16:19	57

Philippians

1:12–13	5, 11
3:14	66

2 Timothy

4:19	57

1 Peter

2:14	35

Bibliography

Albright, William Foxwell and C. S. Mann, eds. *Matthew*. 1st ed. The Anchor Bible. V. 26. Garden City, NY: Doubleday, 1971.

Bauers, Walter, Frederick William Danker, William Arndt, and F. W. Gingrich. *A Greek-English Lexicon of the New Testament and Other Early Christian Literature*. 3rd Edition. Chicago: The University of Chicago Press, 2000.

Bock, Darrell I. *Acts*. Baker Exegetical Commentary on the New Testament. Grand Rapids, MI: Baker Academic, 2007.

---. *Luke*. Baker Exegetical Commentary on the New Testament. Grand Rapids, MI: Baker Books, 1994.

Bruce, F. F. *The Book of Acts*. The New International Commentary on the New Testament. Grand Rapids, MI: W. B. Eerdmans Publishing, 1988.

Chastain, Judson. "The Roman Centurion in the New Testament." PhD. diss., The Southern Baptist Theological Seminary, 1932.

D'Amato, Raffaele. *Roman Centurions 31 BC – AD 500: The Classical and Late Empire*. Oxford: Osprey Publishing, 2012.

Dando-Collins, Stephen. *Legions of Rome: The Definitive History of Every Imperial Roman Legion*. New York: Thomas Dunne Books, 2012.

Davies, Glenn N. "When Was Cornelius Saved?" *The Reformed Theological Review* 46, no. 2 (May 1987): 43–49.

Easter, Matthew C. "'Certainly This Man Was Righteous': Highlighting a Messianic Reading of the Centurion's Confession in Luke 23:47." Tyndale Bulletin 63, no 1 (2012): 35–51.

Edwards, James R. *A Gospel According to Mark*. The Pillar New Testament Commentary. Grand Rapids, MI: Eerdmans, 2002.

Fitzmyer, Joseph A. *The Gospel According to Luke: Introduction, Translation, and Notes*. 1st ed. The Anchor Bible. V. 28–28a. Garden City, NY: Doubleday, 1981.

---. *The Acts of the Apostles*. 1st ed. The Anchor Bible. V. 31. Garden City, NY: Doubleday, 1998.

Flavius Vegetius Renatus. *De Re Militari (Concerning Military Affairs): The Classic Treatise on Warfare at the Pinnacle of the Roman Empire's Power*. London: UK: Leonaur, 2012.

Goldsworthy, Adrian. *The Complete Roman Army*. London: Thames and Hudson, 2011.

---. *The Roman Army at War 100 BC – AD 200*. Oxford: Clarendon Press, 1998.

Green, Joel B. *The Gospel of Luke*. The New International Commentary on the New Testament. Grand Rapids, MI: W. B. Eerdmans Publishing, 1997.

Gundry, Robert. *Matthew: A Commentary on His Literary and Theological Art*. Grand Rapids: MI: Eerdmans, 1982.

Haykin, Michael. A. G. "The Ancient Church in its Graeco-Roman Context." Lecture Series, The Southern Baptist Theological Seminary, Louisville, KY, Fall 2018.

Howell, Justin R. "The Imperial Authority and Benefaction of Centurions and Acts 10:34–43: A Response to C. Kavin Rowe." *Journal for the Study of the New Testament* 31, no. 1 (September 2008): 25–51.

Hunt, A. S. and C. C. Edgar, trans. *Select Papyri, Volume II: Public Documents*. Loeb Classical Library. Cambridge, MA: Harvard University Press, 1934.

Iosif, Despina. *Early Christian Attitudes to War and Military Service*. Piscataway, NJ: Gorgias Press, 2013.

Jeffers, James S. *The Greco-Roman World of the New Testament Era: Exploring the Background of Early Christianity*. Downers Grove, IL: IVP Academic, 1999.

Jennings, Theodore W. and Tat-Siong Benny Liew. "Mistaken Identities but Model Faith: Rereading the Centurion, the Chap and the Christ in Matthew 8:5-13." *Journal of Biblical Literature* 123, no. 3 (September 2004): 467-494.

Josephus. *The Jewish War: Books 1-7*. Ed. Jeffery Henderson, T. E. Page, E. Capps, and W. H. D. Rouse. Trans. H. St. J. Thackeray. Loeb Classical Library. Cambridge, MA: Harvard University Press, 1927-1928.Rankov, Boris. *The Praetorian Guard*. Oxford: Osprey Publishing, 1994.

Julius Caesar. *Civil War*. Ed. and Trans. Cynthia Damon. Loeb Classical Library. Cambridge, MA: Harvard University Press, 2016.

---. *The Gallic War*. Trans. H. J. Edwards. Loeb Classical Library. Cambridge, MA: Harvard University Press, 1971.

Lane, William L. *The Gospel of Mark*. New International Commentary on the New Testament. Grand Rapids, MI: William B. Eerdmans Publishing Company, 1974.

Livy. *History of Rome Volume XI: Books 38-40*. Ed. and Trans. J. C. Yardley. Loeb Classical Library. Cambridge, MA: Harvard University Press, 2018.

McKnight, Scott. "Proselytism and Godfearers." *Dictionary of New Testament Background*. Eds. Craig A. Evans and Stanley E. Porter. Downers Grove, IL: Intervarsity Press, 2000.

McRay, J. R. "Caesarea Maritima." *Dictionary of New Testament Background*. Eds. Craig A. Evans and Stanley E. Porter. Downers Grove, IL: Intervarsity Press, 2000.

Osborne, Grant R. Matthew. Zondervan Exegetical Commentary on the New Testament. Volume 1. Ed. Clinton E. Arnold. Grand Rapids, MI: Zondervan, 2010.

Perkin, Hazel W. "God-Fearer." *Baker Encyclopedia of the Bible.* Grand Rapids, MI: Baker Book House, 1988.

Philo. *Every Good Man is Free. On the Contemplative Life. On the Eternity of the World. Against Flaccus. Apology for the Jews. On Providence.* Trans. F. H. Colson. Loeb Classical Library. Cambridge, MA: Harvard University Press, 1941.

Rainey, Anson F. and R. Steven Notley. *The Sacred Bridge: Carta's Atlas of the Biblical World.* Second Emended & Enhanced Edition. Jerusalem: Carta, 2014.

Saddington, D. B. "The Centurion in Matthew 8:5-13: Considering the Proposal of Theodore W. Jennings Jr., and Tat-Siong Benny Lew." *Journal of Biblical Literature* 125, no. 1 (2006): 140-142.

Shatzman, Israel. *The Armies of the Hasmonaeans and Herod: From Hellenistic to Roman Frameworks.* Heidelberg: Mohr Siebeck, 1991.

Strauss, Mark L. *Mark.* Zondervan Exegetical Commentary on the New Testament. Volume 2. Ed. Clinton E. Arnold. Grand Rapids, MI: Zondervan, 2014.

Turner, David L. *Matthew.* Baker Exegetical Commentary on the New Testament. Grand Rapids, MI: Baker Academic, 2008.

www.ingramcontent.com/pod-product-compliance
Lightning Source LLC
Chambersburg PA
CBHW030308100526
44590CB00012B/567